A History of Uzbekistan

September 2025

Malika Nazarova

Table of Contents

- **Introduction**

- **Chapter 1** The Ancient Oasis Civilizations: Bactria, Sogdiana, and Khwarazm

- **Chapter 2** Under Achaemenid and Hellenistic Rule

- **Chapter 3** The Kushan Empire and the Flourishing of the Silk Road

- **Chapter 4** The Arrival of the Turks and the Western Turkic Khaganate

- **Chapter 5** The Arab Conquest and the Introduction of Islam

- **Chapter 6** The Golden Age of the Samanids

- **Chapter 7** The Rise of Turkic Dynasties: Ghaznavids and Karakhanids

- **Chapter 8** The Khwarazmian Empire and its Dominion

- **Chapter 9** The Mongol Invasion and its Aftermath

- **Chapter 10** The Chagatai Khanate and the Rise of Turco-Mongol Traditions

- **Chapter 11** Amir Timur and the Timurid Empire: A Central Asian Renaissance

- **Chapter 12** The Legacy of Ulugh Beg and the Timurid Decline

- **Chapter 13** The Shaybanids and the Establishment of Uzbek Khanates

- **Chapter 14** The Khanate of Bukhara: A Center of Islamic Learning

- **Chapter 15** The Khanates of Khiva and Kokand: Rival Powers in the Region

- **Chapter 16** The Russian Conquest of Central Asia

- **Chapter 17** Life Under Tsarist Rule and the Jadidist Movement

- **Chapter 18** The Russian Revolution and the Basmachi Revolt

- **Chapter 19** The Creation of the Uzbek Soviet Socialist Republic

- **Chapter 20** Soviet Modernization and its Impact on Uzbek Society

- **Chapter 21** Uzbekistan During the Second World War and the Post-War Era

- **Chapter 22** The Path to Independence: The Late Soviet Years

- **Chapter 23** The First Years of Independence under Islam Karimov

- **Chapter 24** Navigating Regional and Global Politics in the 21st Century

- **Chapter 25** The Mirziyoyev Era: A New Chapter of Reforms and Openness

Introduction

To speak of a history of Uzbekistan is to speak of a history of the world. This is no mere hyperbole, but a recognition of the land's enduring role as a pivotal crossroads of civilizations. For millennia, the territory that constitutes modern-day Uzbekistan has been a stage upon which the grand dramas of empires, religions, and cultures have unfolded. Situated in the heart of Central Asia, it is a doubly landlocked nation, a country surrounded by other landlocked countries, a geographical fact that belies its profound and lasting connectedness to the far corners of the globe. From the fertile river valleys that nurtured some of the region's earliest settled civilizations to the formidable mountain ranges that channeled the flow of trade and conquest, the geography of Uzbekistan has been a defining force in its story.

This is a land that has been known by many names over the centuries: Transoxiana, the land "beyond the Oxus River" to the Greeks and Romans; Mawarannahr, "that which is beyond the river" to the Arab conquerors; and Turkestan, the domain of Turkic peoples. Each name reflects a different era, a different ruling power, a different cultural orientation. But through all these changes, one constant has remained: its role as a dynamic center of exchange. The fabled Silk Road, that vast and ancient network of trade routes connecting East and West, was not merely a path that passed through this land; its very heart beat in the oasis cities of Samarkand, Bukhara, and Khiva. Here, caravans laden with silk, spices, precious metals, and porcelain paused and traded, but they exchanged more than mere commodities. They exchanged ideas, technologies, artistic styles, and religious beliefs, creating a vibrant, cosmopolitan milieu that was unique in the ancient world.

The story of Uzbekistan is therefore a story of layers, of successive waves of peoples and cultures, each leaving its indelible mark on the landscape and the collective identity of its inhabitants. The earliest known settlers were Eastern Iranian peoples, including the Scythians, who established ancient kingdoms in regions like

Bactria, Sogdiana, and Khwarazm. These early civilizations developed sophisticated irrigation systems, transforming the arid plains into flourishing agricultural centers and giving rise to prosperous cities that would become legendary. It was in this crucible of early settlement and innovation that the foundations of a rich and complex society were laid, one that would prove both resilient and adaptable in the face of the many changes to come.

The parade of empires that sought to control this strategic territory is a testament to its enduring importance. The Achaemenid Persians, the conquering armies of Alexander the Great, the Seleucids, the Greco-Bactrians, and the Kushans all held sway, each contributing to the region's diverse cultural and genetic tapestry. The arrival of Turkic peoples from the north and east initiated a demographic and linguistic shift that would profoundly shape the future of the region. The subsequent Arab conquests in the eighth century introduced Islam, a faith that would become a cornerstone of the region's identity and a powerful force in its cultural and intellectual development. The Islamic Golden Age found fertile ground here, with cities like Bukhara and Samarkand emerging as major centers of learning, science, and the arts, producing scholars whose contributions would influence the course of human knowledge.

This history is also one of dramatic and often violent upheaval. The devastating Mongol invasions of the thirteenth century under Genghis Khan brought widespread destruction but also paved the way for new political and cultural configurations. It was from the ashes of the Mongol conquests that one of history's most formidable figures, Amir Timur, or Tamerlane, emerged in the fourteenth century. From his magnificent capital in Samarkand, Timur forged a vast empire and initiated a period of extraordinary artistic and architectural achievement, a renaissance whose stunning mosques, madrasas, and mausoleums continue to inspire awe. The Timurid dynasty he founded, despite its internal struggles, cultivated a refined culture of arts and sciences, most notably under the scholarly rule of his grandson, Ulugh Beg.

The eventual decline of the Timurids gave rise to the Shaybanids, Uzbek Turkic tribes who would give the nation its modern name and establish the khanates of Bukhara, Khiva, and later Kokand. For centuries, these rival khanates dominated the political landscape, fostering distinct cultural and religious traditions while engaging in constant power struggles. This period of fragmentation and internal rivalry eventually left the region vulnerable to the expanding ambitions of a new northern power. The nineteenth century witnessed the gradual and often brutal conquest of Central Asia by the Russian Empire, marking a dramatic turning point in Uzbekistan's history. Tsarist rule brought new technologies, new forms of administration, and new economic realities, but it also imposed a colonial order that would have lasting consequences.

The tumultuous twentieth century brought even more radical change. The Russian Revolution and the establishment of the Soviet Union led to the creation of the Uzbek Soviet Socialist Republic, a redrawing of political boundaries that both reflected and reshaped ethnic and national identities. The Soviet era was a period of contradictions: rapid industrialization, the collectivization of agriculture, and dramatic increases in literacy coexisted with political repression, the suppression of religious and cultural traditions, and environmental catastrophes like the shrinking of the Aral Sea. When the Soviet Union collapsed in 1991, Uzbekistan, for the first time in its modern history, became an independent and sovereign nation.

The journey since independence has been a complex one, marked by the challenges of nation-building, economic transition, and the search for a new place in a rapidly changing world. It is a story of navigating the legacies of its Soviet past while rediscovering and redefining its deeper historical and cultural roots. From the ancient Zoroastrian rituals of the Sogdians to the vibrant Islamic scholarship of the Samanids, from the Turco-Mongol traditions of Timur to the complex social engineering of the Soviet Union, the history of Uzbekistan is a rich and multifaceted narrative. It is a history that is not only of interest in its own right but also offers profound insights into the broader patterns of human civilization, the rise and fall of empires, the transmission of ideas, and the enduring power of culture. This book aims to tell that story, to trace the long and fascinating journey of the land and its people from the ancient oases to the modern nation-state, exploring the triumphs and tragedies, the continuities and the transformations, that have shaped the history of Uzbekistan.

CHAPTER ONE: The Ancient Oasis Civilizations: Bactria, Sogdiana, and Khwarazm

Before the land was Uzbekistan, before the Silk Road carved its legendary path, and before the tread of Achaemenid, Greek, or Arab armies echoed in its valleys, great civilizations had already risen and fallen in the fertile river oases of Central Asia. Their story is not one of a single, unified kingdom, but of a trio of distinct and vibrant cultures, nurtured by the life-giving waters of the Amu Darya and Zeravshan rivers. These were the realms of Bactria, Sogdiana, and Khwarazm, the foundational pillars of a settled, urban life in a region often defined by the vast, open steppe. Their people, primarily of Eastern Iranian stock, were pioneers who mastered the arid landscape, building a world of prosperous cities and verdant fields that would become a coveted prize for future empires.

The engine of these societies was water. In the seemingly inhospitable expanse between the great Kyzylkum and Karakum deserts, the Amu Darya, known to the ancient Greeks as the Oxus, and the Syr Darya, or Jaxartes, provided the means for life. Harnessing these powerful rivers and their tributaries through complex irrigation canals, these early inhabitants transformed desert fringes into agricultural heartlands. This mastery of hydraulic engineering allowed for the cultivation of wheat and barley, sustaining growing populations and freeing a portion of society to pursue other crafts: metallurgy, pottery, and the construction of monumental buildings. It was this agricultural surplus that laid the groundwork for the emergence of a complex, stratified society during the Bronze Age.

The most spectacular manifestation of this early flourishing was a culture so significant and widespread that archaeologists have named it the Bactria-Margiana Archaeological Complex (BMAC), or more evocatively, the Oxus Civilization. Flourishing from around 2400 to 1600 BCE, the BMAC spanned a vast area encompassing modern-day northern Afghanistan, eastern Turkmenistan, southern Uzbekistan, and western Tajikistan. This was not a primitive society of scattered villages, but a network of fortified urban centers, each with its own monumental architecture, workshops, and distinct residential areas. The people of the Oxus Civilization were skilled metalworkers, casting intricate objects in bronze, and their potters produced a variety of distinctive, wheel-turned ceramics.

Bactria, centered on the upper Amu Darya, formed the eastern heartland of the BMAC. Its ancient inhabitants, the Bactrians, were the direct descendants of this Bronze Age culture. Archaeological sites within southern Uzbekistan, such as Sappalli-Tepa and the far larger Djarkutan, reveal the sophistication of this civilization. These were not mere settlements but true proto-cities, planned with defensive walls, temples, and palaces. At Djarkutan, archaeologists uncovered a large temple complex with a fire altar, suggesting religious practices that are widely considered to be a forerunner of Zoroastrianism. This ancient faith, with its dualistic worldview of a constant struggle between good and evil, appears to have deep roots in the region.

The economy of Bactria was firmly rooted in its irrigated fields, but its strategic location also made it a vital hub for trade long before the Silk Road was formally established. The nearby mountains of Badakhshan were the ancient world's primary source of lapis lazuli, a deep blue stone prized by civilizations from Egypt to Mesopotamia. Bactrian traders likely controlled the early stages of this lucrative trade, giving them connections to the great powers of the Near East. The discovery of a single Indus Valley seal and etched carnelian beads at BMAC sites points to established, if indirect, contact with the Harappan civilization to the southeast.

While a distinct writing system for the BMAC has yet to be discovered, they possessed a rich symbolic world expressed through intricately carved stone amulets and seals. These objects, depicting mythical creatures, geometric patterns, and scenes of what may be rituals, offer tantalizing glimpses into their beliefs and social structure. They suggest a society with a priestly class and a ruling elite capable of marshalling the considerable labor required to build and maintain their cities and canal systems. The impressive fortifications surrounding their settlements also speak to a world where defense was a serious concern, a testament to the constant interplay between the settled oasis dwellers and the nomadic peoples of the northern steppes.

North of Bactria, nestled in the fertile valley of the Zeravshan River, lay the land of Sogdiana. This region, destined to give rise to the legendary cities of Samarkand and Bukhara, was home to the Sogdians, another Eastern Iranian people whose name would one day become synonymous with long-distance trade. While the Bronze Age origins of Sogdiana are less dramatically represented than those of the BMAC, its importance grew steadily throughout the Iron Age. The Sogdians were, first and foremost, master agriculturalists, cultivating the rich alluvial soils of the Zeravshan valley.

The proto-urban site of Sarazm, located in modern-day Tajikistan near the Uzbek border, provides a crucial window into the early development of this region. Dating back to the 4th millennium BCE, Sarazm is a UNESCO World Heritage site that demonstrates the existence of a sophisticated, settled culture with far-reaching trade connections long before the rise of Bactria to the south. Archaeologists there have found evidence of advanced metallurgy and craftsmanship, along with goods sourced from as far away as the Iranian plateau and the Indus Valley. This indicates that Sogdiana was never an isolated backwater but was integrated into a network of exchange from its earliest days.

As Sogdiana entered the Iron Age, its settlements evolved. Small communities grew into larger, fortified towns, establishing the pattern of oasis city-states that would characterize the region for centuries. These were politically independent entities, each controlling a slice of irrigated land and competing for resources and trade advantages. Unlike the sprawling, centralized structures of the BMAC, Sogdiana's early political landscape was likely more fragmented, a collection of local principalities ruled by a landed aristocracy. Their primary interactions were with each other and with the nomadic Saka (Scythian) tribes who roamed the steppes to their north and east.

This relationship with the nomads was complex and defining. It was a symbiotic dance of conflict and commerce. Nomadic groups might raid the agricultural settlements, but they were also crucial trading partners, supplying livestock, leather, and furs in exchange for grain, textiles, and crafted goods. This constant interaction shaped Sogdian society, forcing them to be resilient and adaptable, skilled in both defense and diplomacy. It was on this anvil of oasis agriculture and steppe interaction that the pragmatic and resourceful Sogdian character was forged, laying the foundation for their future role as the master merchants of Central Asia.

The third great center of ancient civilization was Khwarazm, a large and fertile oasis located in the Amu Darya delta, just south of the Aral Sea. Geographically more isolated than Bactria and Sogdiana, Khwarazm developed a fiercely independent and distinctive culture. Its landscape, a labyrinth of shifting river channels and marshes, presented unique challenges. Survival and prosperity depended on an even more monumental scale of water management, requiring the construction of massive dikes and canals to control the Amu Darya's unpredictable floods and channel its water to their fields. This necessity bred a population of exceptional engineers and collective organizers.

The name Khwarazm itself is ancient, possibly meaning "lowland" or "fertile land," and is mentioned in the Avesta, the holy book of Zoroastrianism. Indeed, many scholars believe that Khwarazm, due to its relative isolation which made it a "preserve of ancient Eastern traditions," may have been the original homeland of the prophet Zoroaster and the birthplace of his religion. The archaeological record lends some support to this idea, with numerous sites revealing evidence of fire worship and burial practices consistent with early Zoroastrian beliefs.

During the early Iron Age, Khwarazm became known to archaeologists as the "land of a thousand fortresses." This is no exaggeration. The landscape is dotted with the ruins of powerful, mudbrick fortresses, testament to a centralized state capable of mobilizing enormous resources for defense. Sites like Koi Krylgan Kala, a unique circular fortress that may have served as a royal sanctuary and astronomical observatory, and the later, sprawling city of Toprak-Kala, reveal a sophisticated urban society with a clear social hierarchy. Their monumental art and architecture show a style distinct from that of Bactria and Sogdiana, with influences that suggest connections to the nomadic art of the steppes as well as to the civilizations of the south.

The society that built these fortresses was ruled by a line of local kings, the Khwarazmshahs, a title that would persist for nearly two millennia. They presided over a productive agricultural economy and a culture that, while sharing a common Iranian heritage with its neighbors, charted its own course. Khwarazm's isolation meant it was less directly affected by the early imperial expansions from Persia, allowing its unique traditions to flourish. The Khwarazmians were a proud and resilient people, their identity forged by the demands of taming their river delta environment and the necessity of defending it from outsiders.

Before the dawn of the first Persian Empire, therefore, the lands of modern Uzbekistan were not an empty stage but a thriving and complex world. The peoples of Bactria, Sogdiana, and Khwarazm had already established deep roots, creating prosperous societies based on sophisticated irrigation agriculture. They were culturally and linguistically related, part of the broader Eastern Iranian world, yet each had developed its own distinct political and social structures. Bactria was a land of large, ancient cities with connections to the great Bronze Age civilizations. Sogdiana was a patchwork of dynamic city-states in a fertile river valley, honing the commercial skills that would later define them. Khwarazm was a powerful and isolated kingdom of fortress builders and engineers, creators of a unique and enduring culture in the Amu Darya delta. It was upon this rich and ancient foundation that the next chapter of history, the age of empires, would be written.

CHAPTER TWO: Under Achaemenid and Hellenistic Rule

The patchwork of oasis kingdoms in Bactria, Sogdiana, and Khwarazm, accustomed to a delicate balance of trade and conflict with their nomadic neighbors, was soon to be absorbed into a geopolitical entity of an entirely different scale. To their south, in the highlands of Persia, a new power was stirring. The Achaemenid Empire, founded by the visionary Cyrus the Great, was embarking on a course of conquest that would create the largest empire the world had yet seen. For the peoples of Central Asia, this marked the end of an era of relative isolation and the beginning of their integration into the wider political and economic world of the Near East.

The Achaemenid incorporation of the region seems to have been a gradual process, beginning in the 540s BCE. Cyrus, having consolidated his rule over the Median and Lydian kingdoms, turned his seemingly inexhaustible energies eastward. The ancient Bactrians, perhaps recognizing the futility of resistance against such a formidable force, are said by some sources to have submitted voluntarily. Sogdiana and the more remote Khwarazm were also brought into the imperial fold. For the first time, these disparate but culturally related territories were united under a single, overarching political authority, a super-state that stretched from the Aegean Sea to the Indus River.

This new reality was not without its perils. The northern frontiers, bordering the vast Eurasian steppe, remained a source of instability. Cyrus himself would meet his end in this region, a cautionary tale for all future emperors who sought to tame the fierce nomadic tribes. The Greek historian Herodotus tells a vivid, if possibly embellished, story of Cyrus's final campaign in 530 BCE against the Massagetae, a powerful confederation of steppe peoples living east of the Aral Sea. Led by their formidable queen, Tomyris, the Massagetae proved a fatal challenge. Lured into a trap and defeated, Cyrus was killed. Herodotus claims the vengeful queen had his corpse decapitated and the head plunged into a wineskin filled with blood, a grim fulfillment of her promise to quench his thirst for conquest. While other accounts of his death exist, the message was clear: Central Asia's northern frontier was not a line on a map but a turbulent zone of interaction that could humble even the greatest of kings.

Under Cyrus's successors, particularly Darius I, the Achaemenid administration was formalized. The empire was divided into satrapies, or provinces, each governed by a satrap who answered to the Great King. Bactria became one of the most important of these eastern satrapies, a vast and wealthy province often entrusted to a close relative of the king. Its strategic importance and agricultural wealth made it a cornerstone of Achaemenid power in the east. Sogdiana was initially administered as part of the Bactrian satrapy, while Khwarazm, though listed as a subject nation, appears to have enjoyed a greater degree of autonomy due to its geographic isolation.

Life under Achaemenid rule brought profound changes. The most significant was the region's incorporation into a vast, unified economic zone. The Royal Road, the empire's famous highway, facilitated communication and trade, even if its main arteries lay further south. A standardized currency, the gold daric and silver siglos, smoothed commercial transactions. For the Sogdians, in particular, this new imperial framework provided a secure environment in which their innate mercantile skills could flourish. They began to establish trading colonies far beyond their homeland, a precursor to their later dominance of the Silk Road.

The peoples of Central Asia were now expected to pay tribute and provide soldiers for the Great King's armies. The great rock-carved Behistun Inscription of Darius I, which lists the peoples subject to his rule, proudly names the Bactrians, Sogdians, and Khwarazmians. Soldiers from the region would fight in the epic Persian Wars against the Greeks. Herodotus describes the Bactrian cavalry and infantry, clad in their distinctive trousers and armed with cane bows, serving in the massive army of Xerxes. This military service, while a burden, also exposed the local elites to the wider world of the empire, its technologies, and its ideas.

Culturally, the Achaemenid influence was more of a reinforcement than a revolution. Zoroastrianism, with its roots deep in the region's Bronze Age past, was the official religion of the Achaemenid court. Imperial patronage likely strengthened its hold and standardized certain rituals, but the core beliefs were already familiar. The empire practiced a relatively tolerant policy towards local customs and religions, more concerned with loyalty, tribute, and military levies than with imposing cultural uniformity. Achaemenid art and architecture made their mark, particularly in administrative centers, but local traditions continued to thrive.

The Pax Persica, or Persian Peace, was not always peaceful. The accession of new kings was often a trigger for rebellion in distant provinces, and Central Asia was no exception. Records speak of rebellions in Bactria that had to be suppressed by Achaemenid armies. The satraps themselves, often powerful figures with royal blood, could harbor their own ambitions. Yet for over two centuries, the Achaemenid framework held, bringing a measure of stability and connecting the oasis civilizations to a world larger than they had ever known. This period of relative tranquility, however, was about to be shattered by the arrival of a new, unstoppable force from the west.

In 334 BCE, a young and brilliant Macedonian king named Alexander crossed the Hellespont into Asia. His goal was not merely to punish the Persians for past grievances but to conquer their empire in its entirety. In a series of stunning victories at the Granicus, Issus, and finally at Gaugamela in 331 BCE, Alexander crushed the armies of the last Achaemenid Great King, Darius III. The Persian heartland fell, and Darius fled eastward, hoping to rally support in the still-loyal satrapies of Central Asia.

His chief supporter in this desperate endeavor was Bessus, the satrap of Bactria and a relative of the king. As Alexander and his Macedonian army marched in relentless pursuit, Darius's authority crumbled. In mid-330 BCE, near modern-day Shahrud in Iran,

Bessus and a group of co-conspirators decided that a live, defeated king was more of a liability than a dead one. They betrayed Darius, stabbing him and leaving him to die in a wagon, where he was soon found by Alexander's soldiers. Bessus then fled north, across the Hindu Kush mountains into Bactria, where he declared himself the new Great King, taking the throne name Artaxerxes V.

For Alexander, this was an intolerable act of usurpation. The pursuit of Bessus became a personal quest and the driving force behind his campaign into Central Asia. Crossing the formidable Hindu Kush in the spring of 329 BCE, an epic feat of logistics and endurance, he brought his army into the lands of Bactria. Bessus, who had expected the mountains to be an impassable barrier, panicked. His support evaporated, and he fled across the Oxus River into Sogdiana. Alexander pressed on, establishing his base at Maracanda, the ancient capital of Sogdiana, which would one day be known as Samarkand.

Soon after, Bessus was betrayed by his own Sogdian allies, notably a chieftain named Spitamenes. The usurper was captured, flogged, and handed over to the Macedonians. Alexander, never one for leniency with rivals, had him brutally executed. He may have believed that with the death of Bessus, the conquest of the east was complete. He was sorely mistaken. The capture of the self-proclaimed king did not pacify the region; instead, it unleashed the full force of local resistance. The real war for Central Asia was just beginning.

The conflict that followed was unlike anything Alexander had previously experienced. In Persia and Mesopotamia, he had fought set-piece battles against organized armies. In Bactria and Sogdiana, he faced a fierce, two-year-long guerrilla war. The local lords, accustomed to independence and skilled in mobile warfare, were not prepared to simply swap one foreign master for another. Their leader was the same Spitamenes who had betrayed Bessus. A brilliant and elusive tactician, Spitamenes would prove to be one of the most dangerous adversaries Alexander ever faced.

Spitamenes's strategy was one of hit-and-run raids, ambushes, and popular uprisings. He would strike at isolated Macedonian garrisons and supply lines before melting back into the countryside or seeking refuge with nomadic Scythian allies across the Jaxartes River (Syr Darya). He inflicted several sharp defeats on the Macedonians, annihilating one detachment sent to relieve the besieged garrison at Maracanda. The war became a brutal cycle of rebellion and repression. Alexander, infuriated by this stubborn resistance, responded with overwhelming force, storming and destroying cities, including Cyropolis, and carrying out massacres to terrorize the population into submission.

To secure his northern frontier against Scythian incursions and to serve as a permanent bastion of Greek power, Alexander founded a new city on the banks of the Jaxartes in 329 BCE. He named it Alexandria Eschate, "Alexandria the Farthest," a clear statement of his imperial reach. This city, located in the vicinity of modern Khujand, was one of several military colonies he established in the region to plant a permanent Greco-Macedonian presence. These new settlements were populated by army veterans and forcibly relocated local peoples, designed to be centers of Hellenic culture and military control.

The turning point in the grueling war came through a combination of relentless military pressure and astute political maneuvering. Alexander understood that conquest could not be maintained by force alone. He began a policy of reconciliation, incorporating local nobles into his administration and army. His most significant gesture in this regard was his marriage in 327 BCE to Roxana, the daughter of a captured Sogdian nobleman named Oxyartes. While ancient historians write of Alexander being captivated by her beauty, the marriage was a calculated political act designed to heal the wounds of war and legitimize his rule by binding his dynasty to the local aristocracy.

This policy of fusion began to bear fruit. The Sogdian nobles grew weary of the endless conflict and the devastation it brought to their lands. Spitamenes, increasingly isolated, was finally defeated in battle in 328 BCE. Fleeing to his nomadic allies, he was betrayed once more. They killed him and sent his head to Alexander as a peace offering. With the death of its charismatic leader, the Sogdian revolt collapsed.

Alexander's campaign in Central Asia had been the longest, costliest, and most brutal of his career. It had transformed him from a liberator of Greek cities to a ruthless conqueror and a pragmatic empire-builder. He left behind a network of garrisons and new cities, a Greco-Macedonian ruling class, and a legacy of both destruction and creation. He had irrevocably pulled Bactria and Sogdiana into the orbit of the Hellenistic world.

When Alexander died in Babylon in 323 BCE, his vast, newly forged empire immediately began to fracture as his leading generals, the Diadochi or "Successors," fought for control. In the complex partitions and wars that followed, the eastern satrapies, including Bactria and Sogdiana, fell to Seleucus I Nicator, one of Alexander's most capable commanders. By 312 BCE, Seleucus had consolidated his control over the Asian heartland of the empire, from Syria to the borders of India, establishing the Seleucid Empire.

For the Seleucids, Bactria and Sogdiana were remote but valuable possessions. They maintained Alexander's policy of establishing military and civilian colonies, hoping to create a loyal Greco-Macedonian population to anchor their rule. The Greek language became the language of administration, and Hellenistic culture, art, and urban planning were introduced into the oasis cities. However, the sheer distance from the Seleucid capital, first at Babylon and later at Antioch in Syria, made direct rule difficult. The satraps of Bactria, while nominally appointed by the king, often operated with a great deal of independence.

The focus of the Seleucid kings was frequently on their western rivals, particularly the Ptolemaic Kingdom of Egypt, with whom they were engaged in a series of costly wars over control of Syria. This preoccupation with western affairs provided an opportunity for the ambitious satrap of Bactria to assert his independence. Around 250 BCE, the satrap Diodotus I took the momentous step of breaking away from the Seleucid Empire and declaring himself king. This act marked the birth of the independent Greco-Bactrian Kingdom.

The Greco-Bactrian Kingdom was a remarkable and unique political entity, a bastion of Hellenism in the heart of Central Asia. For over a century, a line of Greek kings ruled over a predominantly Iranian population. Their kingdom, centered in Bactria (northern Afghanistan and southern Uzbekistan), at times extended its control over Sogdiana and pushed south across the Hindu Kush to conquer parts of northern India. They created a vibrant and syncretic culture, blending Greek and local traditions in a fascinating fusion.

Our primary source of information for this kingdom comes from its magnificent coinage. The Greco-Bactrian kings produced some of the finest coins of the Hellenistic world, with strikingly realistic portraits of the rulers on one side and depictions of Greek gods like Zeus, Apollo, and Heracles on the other. These coins, stamped with Greek inscriptions, were a powerful projection of their Hellenic identity and royal authority.

Archaeology provides a more tangible glimpse into this lost Greek world. The most stunning evidence comes from the city of Ai-Khanoum, located on the border of modern-day Afghanistan and Tajikistan at the confluence of the Oxus River. Though just outside modern Uzbekistan, Ai-Khanoum is considered the archetypal Greco-Bactrian city and reveals the culture that dominated the entire region. Excavations there uncovered a city with all the hallmarks of a Greek polis: a large palace, a gymnasium for athletic and intellectual training, a theater capable of seating thousands, and temples with Corinthian columns. Greek inscriptions were found, including a set of Delphic maxims brought from Greece, a poignant reminder of their efforts to preserve their cultural heritage so far from their ancestral homeland.

The kingdom faced constant challenges. The Seleucids did not accept its independence lightly. Around 208 BCE, the Seleucid king Antiochus III the Great launched a major expedition to reclaim the east. He besieged the Greco-Bactrian king Euthydemus I in his capital of Bactra for two years. In the end, Euthydemus managed to negotiate a peace, persuading Antiochus that an independent Bactrian kingdom served as a vital buffer, protecting the eastern flank of the Hellenistic world from the growing threat of nomadic peoples from the northern steppes.

It was this pressure from the north that would ultimately prove fatal. The same dynamic that had confronted Cyrus the Great and vexed Alexander now reasserted itself. Migrations of nomadic peoples, primarily the Scythians (Saka) and a powerful confederation known as the Yuezhi, began to press relentlessly on the borders of Sogdiana and Bactria. Weakened by internal power struggles and endless wars of expansion into India, the Greco-Bactrian Kingdom began to crumble. By around 130 BCE, the last Greek king was overthrown, and the cities were overrun by nomadic invaders. The remarkable, century-long experiment of a Greek kingdom in Central Asia had come to an end, paving the way for a new power to rise from the chaos.

CHAPTER THREE: The Kushan Empire and the Flourishing of the Silk Road

The dust had barely settled on the remnants of the Greco-Bactrian Kingdom when a new power, born of upheaval on the far eastern steppes, arrived to claim its inheritance. The collapse of Greek rule in Central Asia was not the work of a single, unified army but the final act of a decades-long migration that had convulsed the region. This domino effect was set in motion far to the east, in the grasslands of modern-day Gansu, China, the homeland of a nomadic pastoralist confederation known to the Chinese as the Yuezhi. For years, the Yuezhi had been a dominant force, trading jade and horses with the kingdoms of China. Their fortunes changed dramatically in 176 BCE, when they suffered a catastrophic defeat at the hands of their aggressive northern neighbors, the Xiongnu.

This defeat fractured the Yuezhi people. One group, the Lesser Yuezhi, moved south, while the main body, the Greater Yuezhi, was forced to abandon its ancestral lands and embark on a desperate trek westward. Their first stop was the Ili Valley, where they displaced the resident Saka tribes, pushing them south towards Bactria. Their respite was brief. Around 132 BCE, a rival nomadic group, the Wusun, in alliance with the ever-present Xiongnu, attacked the Yuezhi and drove them out of the Ili Valley. Once more displaced, the Yuezhi continued their south-westerly migration, passing through the Ferghana Valley and into Sogdiana, finally settling in the lands north of the Oxus River, the very territories recently vacated by the last Greco-Bactrian kings.

For about a century, the Yuezhi controlled this region, transitioning from a purely nomadic existence to a semi-settled one. They ruled from north of the Oxus, while the now-Hellenized cities of Bactria to the south likely paid them tribute. Chinese sources state that the Yuezhi were organized into five principal tribes, or *yabghus*. For a time, these tribes coexisted in a loose confederation, each ruling its own territory. This fragmented political landscape was not destined to last. Sometime in the early 1st century CE, the chief of one of these tribes, the Guishuang, or Kushans, began a campaign to unify his people.

His name was Kujula Kadphises, and he was the architect of the Kushan Empire. Methodically, he subjugated the other four Yuezhi chieftains, forging the five tribes into a single, powerful political entity under his sole command. With the Yuezhi consolidated, Kujula Kadphises led his new Kushan forces south of the Oxus, taking control of Bactria and the Kabul valley. This move marked the formal establishment of the Kushan dynasty. His reign laid the essential groundwork for a state that would soon become one of the four great powers of the ancient world, a contemporary and peer of Rome, Parthia, and Han China.

Kujula Kadphises was succeeded by his son, Vima Takto, who continued the empire's expansionist trajectory, pushing deeper into northwestern India. The Kushans were no longer just a Central Asian power but were becoming a vast, trans-continental empire. The real consolidation of this empire, however, was achieved under the next rulers, Vima Kadphises and, most famously, Kanishka the Great, who ascended the throne around 127 CE. Under these emperors, the Kushan state reached its zenith, a sprawling domain that stretched from the Aral Sea to encompass most of northern India, with its heartland firmly planted in the ancient lands of Bactria and Sogdiana.

The true genius of the Kushan state was not simply its military might, but its pragmatic recognition of its own unique position straddling the major civilizations of Eurasia. The political unity they imposed on this vast territory created an unprecedented zone of security and stability. This Kushan Peace had a transformative effect on the loose network of trade routes crossing the continent, solidifying them into the legendary Silk Road. For the first time, a single political authority controlled the crucial middle section of this route, from the borders of Parthia in the west to the Tarim Basin in the east, where caravans from China arrived.

Under Kushan protection, trade flourished on a scale never seen before. Merchants could travel with a newfound sense of security, fostering direct commercial links between the Roman Empire, which craved Chinese silk, and the Han Dynasty, which desired Roman glass, gold, and other luxury goods. The Kushan realm became the indispensable intermediary. The oasis cities of Sogdiana and Bactria, including the precursor to modern Termez, became bustling cosmopolitan hubs where goods and people from all corners of the known world converged. Hoards of treasure discovered at sites like Begram, one of the Kushan capitals in modern Afghanistan, attest to this vibrant trade, containing Roman glass, Chinese lacquerware, and Indian ivories all in one place.

To facilitate this booming economy, the Kushans introduced a sophisticated and standardized coinage. Initially copying Greek and local designs, they soon developed their own distinctive currency. Vima Kadphises was the first ruler in the region to issue a substantial number of gold coins, a practice likely inspired by the Roman aureus coins that were flowing into his empire through trade. These coins were a powerful tool of both commerce and propaganda. Struck in gold, silver, and copper, they bore the image of the Kushan king on one side and a bewildering array of deities on the reverse. This eclectic pantheon reflected the incredible diversity of the empire and the tolerant, syncretic approach of its rulers.

Nowhere was this fusion of cultures more apparent than in the religious life of the Kushan Empire. The Kushan rulers did not impose a single state religion but instead patronized a variety of faiths practiced by their diverse subjects. Their coins feature deities from the Greek, Roman, Zoroastrian, and Hindu pantheons. Figures like the Greek Heracles, the Iranian fire god Atar, and the Hindu god Shiva all appear on Kushan currency, a clear statement of the empire's multicultural fabric. This policy was not merely one of passive tolerance but of active synthesis, creating a unique cultural environment where different belief systems could interact and blend.

While many faiths coexisted, the Kushan era is most profoundly associated with the flourishing of Buddhism. It was during their rule that the Mahayana school of Buddhism, which viewed the Buddha as a divine savior figure, grew into a major world religion. Kushan emperors, particularly Kanishka, became great patrons of the faith. According to Buddhist tradition, Kanishka convened the Fourth Buddhist Council, an important event that helped to codify Mahayana doctrines. He sponsored the construction of monasteries and stupas throughout his empire, turning cities in Bactria and Gandhara into major centers of Buddhist learning and pilgrimage.

This imperial patronage fueled one of the most remarkable artistic flowerings in the ancient world: the art of Gandhara. Flourishing in the region of modern-day Pakistan and Afghanistan, which formed the southern core of the Kushan empire, this school of art represented a breathtaking fusion of East and West. Using Hellenistic artistic techniques of realism and drapery learned from the legacy of the Greco-Bactrians, Gandharan artists created the first anthropomorphic, or human-form, sculptures of the Buddha. Before this, the Buddha had only been represented by symbols like his footprints or an empty throne. The serene, Apollo-like faces of the Gandharan Buddhas and the detailed, sensitively rendered figures of Bodhisattvas (enlightened beings) became the standard imagery for Mahayana Buddhism as it spread across Asia. Alongside the Gandharan school, a more indigenous style of art flourished at Mathura in India, also under Kushan patronage.

The Kushans managed their diverse empire through a pragmatic administrative system that borrowed from their predecessors. They adopted the Greek alphabet to write their own Eastern Iranian language, Bactrian, making it the official language of the state. This practical adaptation allowed them to create a functioning bureaucracy over a vast, multilingual territory. The title they adopted for their ruler, *Shao-nano-shao* or "King of Kings," was a direct borrowing from the Achaemenid Persians, a clear attempt to position themselves as legitimate heirs to the ancient imperial traditions of the region.

The golden age of the Kushans, however, began to wane by the early 3rd century CE. The empire faced growing external pressures on two fronts. To the west, in Persia, the relatively weak Parthian Empire was overthrown by the aggressive and centralized Sassanian Empire. The early Sassanian kings, particularly Shapur I, launched campaigns eastward, seizing Bactria and other western provinces from the Kushans around 248 CE. In these territories, they established a vassal state ruled by Sassanian governors who took the title *Kushanshah*, or "King of the Kushans."

Around the same time, the Kushan empire split into western and eastern halves following the death of Emperor Vasudeva I. While the western territories fell to the Sassanians, the eastern kingdom, based in the Punjab, held on for a time but was a shadow of its former self. Its control over the lucrative trade routes diminished as new powers rose. By the mid-4th century CE, this eastern remnant was subjugated by the expanding Gupta Empire of India. The final blow came from the north, with the arrival of new waves of nomadic peoples, including the Hephthalites, who would overwhelm the last vestiges of Kushan and Sassanian control in the region. The great Kushan empire, which for over two centuries had been the stable center of the Eurasian world, fragmented and disappeared, creating a power vacuum that would once again transform the political landscape of Central Asia.

CHAPTER FOUR: The Arrival of ahe Turks and the Western Turkic Khaganate

The political fragmentation that followed the demise of the Kushan Empire created a turbulent and unpredictable landscape in Central Asia. Into this power vacuum stepped a new and formidable group of nomadic warriors known as the Hephthalites. Often referred to as the White Huns, their precise ethnic and linguistic origins remain a subject of scholarly debate, with theories pointing towards an Iranian, Turkic, or Hunnic background. Regardless of their ancestry, their impact was immediate and profound. Appearing on the scene in the late 4th and early 5th centuries CE, they swept into the lands of Bactria, which now became known as Tokharistan, and Sogdiana, displacing the last of the Kushan and Sassanian-backed rulers.

The Hephthalites established a powerful nomadic empire that dominated the region for over a century. Their rule was not one of direct administration in the cities and oasis towns. Instead, they superimposed a military aristocracy over the existing social structure, leaving the local Iranian gentry and Sogdian merchant class to manage their own affairs in exchange for substantial tribute. This arrangement, while extractive, allowed the intricate urban and agricultural life of the oases to continue much as it had before. The Hephthalites were primarily a military force, their strength rooted in their cavalry, and their interests lay in controlling trade routes and extracting wealth from the settled populations they had conquered.

Their military prowess made them a dangerous neighbor for the powerful Sassanian Empire to the south. For decades, the two empires were locked in a cycle of conflict and uneasy truces along their shared frontier in modern-day Afghanistan and Turkmenistan. The Hephthalites proved to be more than a match for the Sassanian armies, inflicting several humiliating defeats. The most catastrophic of these came in 484 CE when the Sassanian King of Kings, Peroz I, led a massive army deep into

Hephthalite territory. Lured into a trap, his army was annihilated, and Peroz himself was killed. This victory cemented Hephthalite dominance in the region and forced the Sassanians to pay them a hefty annual tribute for many years, a clear sign of where the balance of power now lay.

The Hephthalite ascendancy, however, was destined to be challenged by the rise of a new and even more dynamic power from the north. In the Altai Mountains of modern-day Mongolia, a confederation of Turkic-speaking tribes was coalescing. Known to the Chinese as the Tujue, these were the people who would give their name to the entire region and forever change its demographic and linguistic trajectory. These were the Göktürks, or "Celestial Turks," who began their recorded history as vassals of a powerful nomadic empire called the Rouran Khaganate, for whom they served as skilled blacksmiths. This role, while subordinate, gave them expertise in metalworking that was crucial for the production of weapons and cavalry equipment.

The architect of the Turkic rise was a charismatic tribal leader named Bumin. Around 552 CE, Bumin, feeling his strength, demanded a royal princess in marriage from his Rouran overlords. The Rouran Khagan contemptuously refused, reportedly sending back a message that referred to Bumin as his "blacksmith slave." This insult was the spark that ignited a full-scale rebellion. Bumin forged alliances with other disaffected tribes and turned on his former masters. In a decisive battle, he shattered the Rouran army, leading their Khagan to commit suicide. On the ruins of the Rouran state, Bumin established the First Turkic Khaganate, proclaiming himself *Illig Qaghan*, or supreme ruler.

The new empire expanded with explosive speed. Bumin, however, died shortly after his great victory. Following Turkic tradition, the vast new domain was partitioned for administrative purposes between his successors. While his son succeeded him as the supreme Khagan in the east, ruling from the sacred Otuken forests in Mongolia, the immensely important western territories were entrusted to Bumin's younger brother, a formidable and brilliant general named Istämi. Holding the title of *Yabghu* (viceroy),

Istämi became the de facto ruler of a vast territory stretching from the Altai Mountains towards the Caspian Sea. It was his conquests that would bring the lands of Uzbekistan directly under Turkic rule.

Istämi's primary strategic objective was the destruction of the Hephthalite Empire, which controlled the wealthiest oases and the most lucrative sections of the Silk Road. In this, he found a willing, if temporary, ally in the Sassanian Empire. The Sassanians, still smarting from their earlier defeats and burdened by tribute payments, saw an opportunity to eliminate their troublesome northeastern neighbors. An alliance was formed. The two great powers launched a coordinated pincer attack on the Hephthalites. Caught between the Turks advancing from the northeast and the Sassanians from the southwest, the Hephthalite kingdom was crushed sometime around 560 CE. Its territories were partitioned between the victors, with the Amu Darya river forming the new boundary between the Turkic Khaganate and the Sassanian Empire. Sogdiana and Tokharistan were now firmly in Turkic hands.

The alliance with Persia was purely one of convenience and quickly soured. The primary source of friction was control over the Silk Road. The Sogdian merchants, now under Turkic protection, wanted to trade their silk directly with the Byzantine Empire, the primary consumer in the West. This would involve bypassing the Sassanian middlemen, who levied heavy taxes on the trade. When the Sassanian king, Khosrow I, refused to allow the Turkic-Sogdian caravans to pass through his territory, Istämi sought a new, more distant ally. He dispatched a Sogdian merchant named Maniah on a groundbreaking diplomatic mission, not through Persia, but north of the Caspian and Black Seas, to open direct relations with the Byzantine court in Constantinople. This embassy was successful, leading to a Byzantine-Turkic alliance aimed at countering their common Sassanian foe. This strategic partnership underscored the new global reality: the Turkic Khaganate was now a major player on the world stage, capable of projecting its influence from the borders of China to the gates of Europe.

For several decades, the Turkic Khaganate remained a unified, transcontinental empire. However, the sheer size of the territory, coupled with the traditional Turkic system of apportioning rule among members of the royal Ashina clan, created inevitable internal strains. Following a series of succession disputes and civil wars, the great empire officially split into two independent states around 603 CE: the Eastern Turkic Khaganate, based in Mongolia, and the Western Turkic Khaganate, which controlled the vast steppes and oasis cities from the Altai to the Volga. It was this Western Turkic Khaganate that would be the dominant political force in the lands of modern Uzbekistan for the next century.

The rule of the Western Turks was pragmatic and, for the most part, highly beneficial for the local population. The Turkic elite were nomads, their power based on vast herds of livestock and highly mobile cavalry armies. They had little interest in the day-to-day administration of cities or the complex management of irrigation canals. Their primary concern was security, control of trade routes, and the collection of taxes. They established their summer and winter headquarters in the grasslands of the Semirechye region, with major centers at Suyab and Navekat in modern-day Kyrgyzstan. From these camps, the Khagan and his court governed their sprawling domain.

This created a remarkably effective system of dual administration. The Turkic Khagan and his military aristocracy provided the overarching political and military framework, ensuring the stability and security of the realm. They pacified the steppes and protected the lucrative caravan routes. The actual running of the cities and agricultural lands, however, was left in the hands of the local Sogdian and Tokharian elites. The Sogdian merchant class, in particular, thrived under Turkic rule. Freed from the interference of rival empires and protected by the military might of the Khagan, they entered a golden age of commerce. Sogdian caravans now traveled the length and breadth of Asia, from China to Byzantium, under the watchful eye of their Turkic overlords.

This symbiotic relationship was the key to the Khaganate's prosperity. The Turks provided the military muscle that made long-distance trade secure, and the Sogdians provided the economic engine that generated immense wealth. Sogdians became indispensable figures in the Turkic court, serving not only as tax collectors and commercial agents but also as diplomats and political advisors. They were the literate bureaucracy that the nomadic state needed to function. The first Turkic inscriptions were written not in a Turkic script, which had yet to be fully developed, but in the Sogdian language and alphabet, a testament to their crucial role in the state's administration. Murals found at Penjikent and Afrasiab (ancient Samarkand) depict Turkic warriors with their distinctive long hair and Sogdian merchants in their fine robes, illustrating the close interaction between the two communities.

The region around modern Tashkent, known then as Chach, became a vital center within the Western Turkic Khaganate. Its fertile oasis, rich in agricultural produce and mineral resources, made it a key economic hub. The Khagans appointed their own governors, known as *tuduns*, to oversee the collection of taxes and ensure the loyalty of the local rulers. The minting of coins in Chach and other Sogdian cities during this period, often bearing a combination of Turkic and Sogdian symbols and titles, reflects this dual system of governance.

The religious landscape of the Western Turkic Khaganate was as diverse as its population. The ruling Turks themselves adhered to their traditional shamanistic faith, Tengrism, which centered on the worship of a supreme sky god, Tengri. They were, however, remarkably tolerant of the faiths of their subjects. In the cities of Sogdiana and the towns of Tokharistan, a multitude of religions coexisted peacefully. Zoroastrianism remained strong among the Sogdian aristocracy, while Buddhism, a legacy of the Kushan era, continued to flourish, particularly in the southern regions around Termez and in the Ferghana Valley. Nestorian Christianity also had a significant presence, its communities spread along the Silk Road, and Manichaeism, another faith of Iranian origin, found followers among the merchant class. The Turkic rulers made no attempt to impose their own beliefs, understanding that the stability of their multicultural empire depended on religious coexistence.

The power of the Western Turkic Khaganate reached its peak in the early 7th century under rulers like Tong Yabghu Qaghan, who expanded his influence deep into modern-day Afghanistan and northern India. Byzantine sources describe him as a great ruler who controlled a vast and wealthy empire. However, the inherent instability of steppe confederations soon began to manifest. The Khaganate was not a centralized state but a loose federation of tribes, and it was plagued by internal rivalries and constant succession struggles.

The greatest external threat, however, came from the east. The newly unified and expansionist Tang Dynasty in China saw the powerful Turkic Khaganates as their primary strategic rivals. The Tang emperors were masters of a "divide and rule" policy, skillfully exploiting the internal conflicts among the Turkic tribes. They supported rival claimants to the Khagan's throne and encouraged rebellions among vassal peoples. Starting in the 640s, the Tang began a series of military campaigns aimed at extending their control over the oasis states of the Tarim Basin, which had been vassals of the Western Turks.

Weakened by incessant internal warfare between two rival tribal factions, the Khaganate could not mount an effective, unified defense against the relentless Tang pressure. In a major campaign in 657 CE, a Tang army under General Su Dingfang inflicted a decisive defeat on the Western Turks, capturing their last independent Khagan. Following this victory, the Tang empire incorporated the territories of the Khaganate into its own administration, establishing a series of protectorates governed by puppet rulers from the Ashina clan.

Direct Chinese rule over such a vast and distant territory proved short-lived. The collapse of the Khaganate's authority did not lead to a stable new order but rather to political chaos. The Turkic tribes, though defeated, were not destroyed. The demise of the unified Khaganate created a power vacuum, and the region fragmented into a mosaic of smaller, competing principalities. Some were ruled by local Turkic chieftains, others by their Sogdian former subjects. A new Turkic tribal confederation, the Turgesh, briefly established its own Khaganate in the Semirechye region. This period of fragmentation and disunity would have profound consequences. With no single, dominant power to defend the region, the rich oasis cities of Transoxiana were left vulnerable to the advance of a new and determined force that was beginning to mass on the southern horizon.

CHAPTER FIVE: The Arab Conquest and the Introduction of Islam

The collapse of the Western Turkic Khaganate in the mid-seventh century did not usher in a new era of unity for the lands of Transoxiana. Instead, it returned the region to its default political state: a complex and competitive mosaic of small, independent principalities. The great oasis cities of Samarkand, Bukhara, and the fertile territories of Chach, Ferghana, and Tokharistan were once again masters of their own destiny, ruled by a local aristocracy of Sogdian merchants and landholders, known as *dihqans*, or by Turkic chieftains who had settled in the area. This fragmentation, while allowing for a vibrant and diverse local culture to flourish, created a critical military weakness. The princes of Transoxiana were rich, but they were not united. They were far more practiced in the art of commercial rivalry than in the craft of collective defense. It was a vulnerability that would be ruthlessly exploited by a new, unstoppable force coalescing far to the southwest.

On the Arabian Peninsula, the new religion of Islam had forged a scattered collection of tribes into a dynamic and expansionist power. Fueled by a potent combination of religious conviction and a desire for the spoils of conquest, Arab armies had erupted out of the desert with breathtaking speed. In a little over a decade, they had shattered the two great powers that had dominated the Near East for centuries. The Byzantine Empire was pushed out of Syria and Egypt, and the mighty Sassanian Empire of Persia was annihilated completely. The last Sassanian king, Yazdegerd III, became a fugitive, fleeing ever eastward before the relentless Arab advance. By the 650s, the Arab armies of the Rashidun Caliphate had conquered the Sassanian heartland, crossed the Iranian plateau, and established themselves in the vast northeastern province of Khurasan. They now stood on the banks of the Amu Darya, the great Oxus River, the traditional boundary of the Iranian world. Across the river lay the wealthy, disunited city-states of Transoxiana, or as the Arabs would call it, *Mawarannahr*—"that which is beyond the river."

The initial Arab forays into Mawarannahr were not a concerted campaign of conquest but rather seasonal raids launched from their new garrison city of Merv in Khurasan. These expeditions, which began in the 660s under the new Umayyad Caliphate, were primarily aimed at reconnaissance and plunder. A governor would lead an army across the river in the summer, attack a city like Bukhara or Samarkand, extract a hefty tribute and a collection of slaves, and then retreat back to the safety of Khurasan before the onset of winter. The Sogdian rulers found it easier to pay these demands than to mount a sustained resistance. They would hand over silver and textiles, promise to behave, and then renounce the agreement as soon as the Arab army had disappeared over the horizon. This pattern of raid, tribute, and reneging continued for several decades, a profitable but ultimately unstable arrangement for both sides.

This phase of tentative probing came to an abrupt end with the appointment of a new governor of Khurasan in 705 CE. His name was Qutayba ibn Muslim al-Bahili, and he was a man of fierce ambition and strategic vision. Qutayba was not interested in temporary tribute; he intended to bring Mawarannahr permanently under the dominion of the Umayyad Caliphate and the faith of Islam. He abandoned the practice of seasonal raiding and embarked on a series of systematic and relentless campaigns designed to break the will of the local rulers and integrate the region into the empire. For the next decade, Qutayba and his Khurasani Arab army would be the unstoppable protagonists in the drama of the conquest.

His first major target was the rich oasis of Bukhara. The city was ruled by a young prince whose mother, the Khatun, held the real power as regent. The Bukharans and their Turkic allies put up a ferocious fight, but Qutayba's disciplined army proved superior. After a bloody siege, the city submitted in 709 CE. Qutayba's policies in Bukhara set the pattern for his future conquests. He imposed a heavy tribute and established an Arab garrison right in the city to prevent future backsliding. More significantly, he took the unprecedented step of forcing the city's residents to give up half of their own homes to be settled by Arab warriors and their families. This created a permanent occupying force inside the walls, making rebellion far more difficult. He also ordered the construction of a grand mosque on the site of a former temple, a clear and powerful statement of the new order. To encourage conversion, he reportedly offered a payment of two dirhams to any local who attended Friday prayers, a pragmatic if unsubtle piece of religious incentivization.

With Bukhara subdued, Qutayba turned his attention to the greatest prize of all: Samarkand. The ruler of Samarkand, a prince named Ghurak, had watched the fall of Bukhara with alarm and tried to maneuver between the competing powers, appealing for aid from both the Turgesh Turks and the Tang Chinese court. But help was too far away. In 712 CE, Qutayba's army arrived at the gates of the magnificent city. The Sogdians of Samarkand, protected by formidable walls, mounted a desperate defense, using powerful siege engines to hurl stones at the Arab attackers. The battle raged for a month before Ghurak, seeing the futility of further resistance, negotiated a surrender.

The terms were harsh. Ghurak had to agree to pay a massive annual tribute and provide a contingent of soldiers for the Arab army. Qutayba marched his troops into the city and, in a highly symbolic act, ordered the destruction of the city's main fire temple and other religious "idols," which likely included statues from Buddhist shrines. The precious metal from these objects was melted down. A mosque was established, and the local Sogdian nobility was, for a time, forbidden from bearing arms. Having humbled the two greatest cities of Sogdiana, Qutayba pushed his campaigns even further, subjugating the kingdom of Khwarazm on the Amu Darya delta and launching a daring raid deep into the Ferghana Valley, reaching the very borders of the Tang Chinese sphere of influence.

The conquest was not a simple, one-sided affair. Resistance was fierce, stubborn, and recurrent. The Sogdian aristocracy did not meekly accept their new masters. As soon as Qutayba's attention was turned elsewhere, cities would rebel, treaties would be broken, and new alliances would be formed with Turkic tribes from the steppes. The most determined resistance was led by Dewashtich, the ruler of the city of Penjikent. Styling himself the "King of Soghd, Lord of Samarkand," he attempted to rally the disparate local forces into a unified front against the invaders. For several years, he led a guerrilla war from his mountain fortress at Mugh, but he was eventually cornered, captured, and executed in 722 CE. His struggle, documented in a remarkable cache of Sogdian-language documents discovered at his fortress, provides a vivid picture of the turmoil and desperation of the local elites.

The greatest external challenge to Arab rule came from the north. The Turgesh, a powerful Turkic confederation that had risen from the ashes of the Western Turkic Khaganate, established their own state in the steppes and saw the Arab advance as a direct threat. Under strong Khagans, the Turgesh became the primary champions of the anti-Arab cause in Mawarannahr, providing military support for Sogdian rebellions. For two decades, the region was engulfed in a brutal back-and-forth war. The Turgesh inflicted several severe defeats on the Umayyad armies. The most notable of these was the disastrous "Day of Thirst" in 724 CE, when an Arab army operating in the Ferghana Valley was ambushed by the Turgesh, cut off from water, and nearly annihilated during its retreat. Another major defeat in 731 CE at the Battle of the Defile saw thousands of Arab soldiers killed. For a time, it seemed as though the Arabs might be pushed out of Mawarannahr altogether.

The tide began to turn with the appointment of a new, more astute governor of Khurasan, Nasr ibn Sayyar, in 738 CE. Nasr realized that military force alone was not enough to pacify the region. He instituted a series of crucial reforms aimed at winning over the local population. He reformed the tax system to make it more equitable, ending the practice of taxing recent converts to Islam, which had been a major source of resentment. He also reached out to the local *dihqan* aristocracy, offering them a place in the new administrative structure and confirming their land ownership in exchange for their loyalty. This policy of co-option was highly effective, gradually eroding the basis for popular rebellion by creating a vested interest in the stability of Arab rule among the local elite. His efforts were aided by the convenient collapse of the Turgesh Khaganate due to internal strife, which deprived the Sogdian rebels of their most powerful external ally.

Just as Arab control was being solidified, a new geopolitical rival entered the scene. The Tang Dynasty of China, at the height of its power, was also pursuing an expansionist policy in Central Asia. The Chinese saw the Arab advance as a challenge to their influence over the petty kingdoms of the region, including Ferghana and Chach. The two superpowers were on a collision course, and the final showdown came in 751 CE on the banks of the Talas River, in present-day Kyrgyzstan. A large Tang Chinese army, commanded by the Korean general Gao Xianzhi, marched west to assert its authority. They were met by a combined force of Arab and local Turkic troops under the command of Ziyad ibn Salih.

The Battle of Talas raged for five days. The decisive moment came when the Karluk Turks, a contingent serving with the Chinese army, switched sides mid-battle and attacked the Tang forces from the rear. This betrayal caused the Chinese lines to collapse into a rout. The Arab-led army won a resounding victory. The battle's consequences were immense. It definitively halted the westward expansion of the Tang Empire and cemented the dominance of Islam in Central Asia for centuries to come. The Tang, soon to be convulsed by the devastating An-Lushan Rebellion, would never again be in a position to project power so far west. An interesting, though possibly apocryphal, side effect of the battle was the capture of Chinese artisans who, according to tradition, brought the secrets of papermaking to the Islamic world, a technology that would have a profound impact on scholarship and administration.

At almost the same moment as the victory at Talas, the wider Islamic world was undergoing a political earthquake. Discontent with the rule of the Damascus-based Umayyad Caliphate had been brewing for years, nowhere more so than in the eastern province of Khurasan. Led by a mysterious figure named Abu Muslim, a revolutionary movement acting in the name of the Abbasid family, relatives of the Prophet Muhammad, harnessed this discontent. Khurasani Arabs, resentful of being treated as provincials by the Syrian elite, and newly converted Iranian and Sogdian Muslims (*mawali*), angry at persistent discrimination, flocked to the black banners of the Abbasid cause. In 750 CE, this revolutionary army marched west, defeated the Umayyads, and established the Abbasid Caliphate.

The Abbasid Revolution had a profound impact on Mawarannahr. The new caliphs moved the capital of the empire from Damascus to a newly founded city in Mesopotamia: Baghdad. This eastward shift ended the dominance of the Arab Syrian aristocracy and brought Iranian and Central Asian peoples into the heart of the imperial administration. Central Asians now played a key role in the government and the army of the caliphate. This integration gave them a greater stake in the success of the empire and helped to reconcile them to Islamic rule.

The arrival of the Arabs and the century-long process of conquest had irrevocably transformed the region. The old political order of independent city-states was gone, replaced by a single imperial authority. A new religion, Islam, was now firmly entrenched as the faith of the ruling class and was steadily gaining converts among the general population, though this process would take centuries to complete. Zoroastrianism, Buddhism, Nestorian Christianity, and Manichaeism did not vanish overnight, but they began a slow decline into minority status. The Arabic language was introduced as the medium of administration and, more importantly, of religious scripture, bringing with it a powerful new intellectual tradition. This process was not one of simple replacement but of synthesis. The rich cultural and intellectual heritage of the ancient Sogdians and Bactrians did not disappear; it was instead fused with the new faith and language to create a unique and vibrant Perso-Islamic civilization, whose golden age was now just over the horizon.

CHAPTER SIX: The Golden Age of the Samanids

The Abbasid Revolution, which had been powered by the soldiers of Khurasan and Mawarannahr, fundamentally reoriented the Islamic world. With the caliphate's capital shifted to Baghdad, the cultural and political center of gravity moved east, away from the Mediterranean focus of the Umayyads. This new proximity to the Iranian heartlands brought a surge of Persian influence into the court, administration, and culture of the empire. For the lands beyond the Oxus, this meant not subjugation but partnership. Central Asians were no longer just conquered subjects on a distant frontier; they were now kingmakers and core constituents of the caliphate. This new status, combined with the immense distance from Baghdad, created the perfect conditions for the emergence of local dynasties that could rule with autonomy while still paying nominal allegiance to the caliphal authority.

The first of these dynasties to establish a semi-independent foothold was the Tahirids, who governed the vast province of Khurasan for the caliphs from the 820s. While their authority sometimes extended into Mawarannahr, their focus remained on cities like Nishapur and Merv. They were, in essence, glorified provincial governors, almost entirely Arabized in their cultural outlook. Their grip on power provided a period of stability but also demonstrated to other ambitious local families that a new political reality was taking shape. The weakening of direct caliphal control created opportunities, and it was from the ranks of the indigenous Iranian landowning aristocracy the *dihqans*—that the next wave of rulers would emerge.

The family that would define this era traced its lineage to one such *dihqan* named Saman Khuda, from the village of Saman near Balkh in modern-day Afghanistan. Claiming descent from the ancient Sassanian nobility, Saman Khuda was a figure of local importance who, in the early eighth century, abandoned his ancestral Zoroastrianism and converted to Islam. His descendants inherited his status and ambition. His four grandsons—Nuh, Ahmad, Yahya, and Ilyas—served the Abbasid caliph al-Ma'mun with loyalty when he was governor of Khurasan. For their faithful service, al-Ma'mun, after becoming caliph, rewarded them with the governorships of key cities. Nuh received Samarkand, Ahmad was granted Ferghana, Yahya took control of Shash (modern Tashkent), and Ilyas was given Herat. For several decades, the brothers and their descendants ruled these territories as loyal vassals of the Abbasids and their Tahirid governors.

The Samanid brothers governed effectively, consolidating their power base and expanding their influence. It was Ahmad's son, Nasr I, who first united most of Mawarannahr under the family's rule. In 875, the Caliph officially recognized him as the governor of the entire region, with his capital in Samarkand. This act formally established the Samanid state, though still technically under the suzerainty of Baghdad. Nasr's authority, however, was soon challenged from within his own family by his more dynamic and capable younger brother, Isma'il. A dispute over the distribution of tax revenue led to a brief civil war, from which Isma'il emerged victorious. Yet, in a shrewd political move, he allowed his brother to retain his title as head of the family until Nasr's death in 892, thereby avoiding any open breach with the caliph who had appointed Nasr.

Upon his brother's death, Isma'il Samani (892–907) took sole command, uniting the Samanid state and moving the capital from Samarkand to Bukhara. It was under his leadership that the dynasty reached its zenith of power and prestige. Isma'il was a brilliant military commander and a far-sighted statesman, the true architect of the Samanid golden age. He secured his northern frontiers by launching a decisive campaign against the Karluk Turks in 893, capturing the city of Talas and extending the reach of both his empire and Sunni Islam deep into the steppe. This campaign also had a vital economic consequence, ensuring a steady supply of Turkic slaves, who would form the formidable backbone of the Samanid army.

His greatest test came from the south. A rival Persian dynasty, the Saffarids, had risen in Sistan and conquered much of modern-day Iran and Afghanistan, deposing the Tahirids in the process. The Saffarid ruler, Amr ibn al-Layth, saw the Samanids as an obstacle to his ambition of unifying the entire Iranian east. The Abbasid caliph, wary of the Saffarids' growing power, played the two dynasties against each other, officially granting Khurasan to Amr while secretly encouraging Isma'il to resist. In the spring of 900, the two armies met near Balkh. Isma'il, though outnumbered, won a stunning victory, capturing Amr ibn al-Layth and sending him in chains to Baghdad, where he was later executed. This victory was a defining moment. It gave the Samanids control over the vast and wealthy province of Khurasan and established them as the undisputed paramount power in the eastern Islamic world, effectively independent of Baghdad in all but name.

With the realm secure, Isma'il and his successors built a sophisticated and prosperous state. The administration was modeled on the Abbasid bureaucracy, with a central chancellery (*divan*) managing affairs of state. While Arabic remained the language of religion and science, the Samanid court pioneered a monumental cultural shift by championing the use of New Persian (also known as Dari or Farsi) as the language of administration and literature. This was not an anti-Arab or anti-Islamic movement but a conscious cultivation of a distinct Perso-Islamic identity. In a famous edict, the Samanids declared that "here, in this region, the language is Persian, and the kings of this realm are Persian kings." This patronage laid the foundation for a spectacular cultural renaissance.

The Samanid state rested on a foundation of economic prosperity. Agriculture thrived in the fertile river valleys, supported by extensive and well-maintained irrigation networks that had been the region's lifeblood for millennia. Commerce was the other pillar of the economy. The political stability provided by the Samanids created a secure environment for trade to flourish. The cities of Bukhara and Samarkand became bustling hubs on the revitalized Silk Road, connecting China with the Middle East and Europe. Samanid merchants also conducted a vigorous trade with the nomadic peoples of the northern steppes, exchanging textiles and metalwork for furs, leather, and, most importantly, slaves. The silver dirhams minted by the Samanids were a stable and widely accepted currency, with hoards of Samanid coins having been discovered as far away as Scandinavia.

This wealth and stability transformed the major cities into glittering centers of civilization. The capital, Bukhara, grew into one of the great metropolises of the Islamic world, a rival in glory to Baghdad itself. It became known as *Bukhara-i-Sharif* ("Noble Bukhara") and the "Dome of Islam" in the East, a testament to its importance as a center of religious and intellectual life. Scholars, poets, artists, and thinkers from across the Muslim world flocked to the Samanid court, drawn by the promise of generous patronage. A magnificent royal library, the *Siwan al-Hikma* ("Storehouse of Wisdom"), was established in Bukhara, housing a vast collection of books on every branch of knowledge.

It was in this vibrant intellectual atmosphere that the Persian literary renaissance blossomed. The Samanid amirs were passionate patrons of poetry, and it was at their court that New Persian was forged into a powerful and elegant literary medium. The undisputed master of this early period was Rudaki, often called the "father of Persian poetry." Though he eventually died in poverty, for years he was the celebrated poet laureate of the court in Bukhara, composing verses of exquisite beauty and setting the standard for generations of poets to come. Another major figure was Daqiqi, who began the monumental task of rendering the pre-Islamic history and legends of Iran into a Persian epic, a project that would later be completed by Ferdowsi in his immortal *Shahnameh*.

The scientific and philosophical achievements of the era were no less brilliant. The Samanid realm nurtured some of the greatest minds in human history. A young physician and philosopher from a village near Bukhara, Abu Ali ibn Sina, known to the West as Avicenna, began his intellectual journey by gaining access to the royal library. His later works, particularly *The Canon of Medicine*, would become foundational texts for medical education in both the

Islamic world and Europe for centuries. Scholars like Abu Rayhan al-Biruni, a polymath of breathtaking genius, and al-Farabi, a towering figure in Islamic philosophy, also benefited from the scholarly environment fostered by the Samanids.

The religious sciences also flourished. Bukhara became a preeminent center for the study of Sunni Islam, particularly the Hanafi school of jurisprudence. It was the birthplace of Imam al-Bukhari, whose compilation of the sayings of the Prophet Muhammad, the *Sahih al-Bukhari*, is considered by Sunni Muslims to be the most authentic collection of hadith and one of the most important books after the Qur'an. The Samanids were staunch promoters of Sunni orthodoxy, and under their rule, the populations of Mawarannahr and Khurasan became more deeply and uniformly Islamicized.

Samanid patronage also extended to architecture and the arts. While much of their architectural legacy in cities like Samarkand was destroyed in later invasions, one supreme masterpiece remains in Bukhara: the mausoleum of Isma'il Samani. Completed in the early tenth century, this small, exquisitely proportioned structure is a marvel of baked brick construction. Its intricate brickwork creates a dynamic interplay of light and shadow, and its perfect cubic form, topped by a central dome, synthesizes pre-Islamic Sogdian and Sassanian architectural motifs with emerging Islamic principles. It stands as a powerful symbol of the confident and creative spirit of the age. Samanid potters, particularly in Samarkand and Nishapur, also produced some of the finest ceramics in the Islamic world, renowned for their elegant forms and striking calligraphic decorations.

The golden age of the Samanids, however, proved to be tragically brief. The very foundations of the state's military power contained the seeds of its destruction. The empire relied heavily on a professional army composed of Turkic slave-soldiers, or *ghulams*. These soldiers, captured or purchased from the northern steppes, were loyal to the person of the amir rather than to the state. While they were formidable warriors, their power grew steadily throughout the tenth century. Ambitious *ghulam* commanders were appointed as governors of provinces and eventually became powerful enough to act as kingmakers, dominating the court and treating the Samanid rulers as mere puppets.

The decline began in the latter half of the tenth century. A succession of weak and ineffectual rulers ascended the throne, unable to control their powerful Turkic generals. In 962, a disgruntled *ghulam* commander named Alptigin seized the remote city of Ghazna and established a semi-independent lordship, which would later evolve into the mighty Ghaznavid Empire under his successors. While figures like Alptigin and his successor Sabuktigin continued to pay lip service to the Samanids, they ruled their territories as independent kings. The state was further weakened by internal revolts, feudal strife, and a series of financial crises that undermined the central government's authority.

The final blow came from a new Turkic power that had emerged on the northeastern frontier. A confederation of Turkic tribes, the Karakhanids, who had recently converted to Islam, saw the crumbling Samanid state as ripe for the taking. Pressing down from the north, they exploited the Samanids' internal weakness. At the same time, the Ghaznavids under Sabuktigin's ambitious son, Mahmud, were pressing up from the south, seizing control of the vital province of Khurasan. Caught in a pincer movement between these two rising Turkic powers, the Samanid state collapsed. In 999, the Karakhanids marched into Bukhara without a fight, taking the last Samanid amir captive. A final, desperate attempt by a Samanid prince, Isma'il Muntasir, to restore the dynasty's fortunes in the early years of the eleventh century ended in his death in 1005. The great Samanid state, which had presided over one of the most brilliant periods of cultural flourishing in Central Asian history, was no more. Its territories were partitioned between the two new Turkic dynasties that would now dominate the region: the Ghaznavids and the Karakhanids.

CHAPTER SEVEN: The Rise of Turkic Dynasties: Ghaznavids and Karakhanids

The final collapse of the Samanid state in the opening years of the eleventh century was not the end of an era so much as the confirmation of a new one. The cultural and religious landscape of Mawarannahr had been profoundly shaped by the Persian-speaking Samanids, but the political and military reality had been trending in a different direction for decades. The reliance on Turkic slave-soldiers, the constant pressure from Turkic tribes on the northern frontier, and the rise of ambitious Turkic generals within the Samanid system had created a world where Turkic military power was the ultimate arbiter of fate. The passing of the Samanids simply swept away the veneer of the old order, revealing the two formidable Turkic powers that had been rising in its shadow: the Karakhanids to the north and the Ghaznavids to the south. Their ascendancy would partition the Samanid inheritance and set the region on a new course, one defined by the fusion of Turkic rule with the established Perso-Islamic culture of the oasis cities.

The first of these powers to burst onto the scene were the Karakhanids, a confederation of Turkic tribes, primarily the Karluks, who had for centuries roamed the steppes of Semirechye and Kashgaria, east of the main Samanid realm. Unlike the Turkic peoples who had entered the Islamic world as individual slaves or mercenaries, the Karakhanids entered it as a sovereign entity, a tribal state that adopted the new religion on its own terms. The pivotal moment came in the mid-tenth century when, according to tradition, their leader Satuq Bughra Khan converted to Islam. This act had immense consequences, transforming the Karakhanids from a confederation of pagan tribes into a legitimate Islamic dynasty, possessed of the religious authority to wage war on their neighbors. They were now ghazis, warriors for the faith, with their eyes set on the rich, civilized, and now politically fragile lands to their west.

For years, they probed the weakening Samanid defenses. The final act was almost anticlimactic. In 999, the Karakhanid ruler Nasr ibn Ali marched his army on Bukhara. The Samanid state was so hollowed out by internal strife and the disloyalty of its own Turkic generals that the city fell without a serious fight. The last Samanid amir was taken captive, and the Karakhanids became the new masters of Mawarannahr. Their domain now encompassed the heartlands of modern Uzbekistan, including the great cities of Bukhara and Samarkand, the fertile Ferghana Valley, and their original territories stretching eastward to Kashgar. The Amu Darya river became the new frontier, a dividing line between the Karakhanid realm and the lands claimed by the other rising Turkic power.

Karakhanid rule represented a significant departure from the centralized, bureaucratic statecraft of the Samanids. Their political structure reflected their nomadic origins. The realm was not seen as a unitary state but as the collective property, or appanage, of the ruling royal family. This led to a system of dual administration, with the territory frequently divided into a senior eastern Khanate based at Balasagun and a junior western Khanate ruling over Mawarannahr from Bukhara or Samarkand. Authority was further subdivided among various members of the royal clan, each of whom held a title corresponding to their rank in the hierarchy and governed their own allotted territory. While this system provided a measure of autonomy for different branches of the family, it was also a recipe for chronic instability. The history of the Karakhanid state is a bewildering saga of internecine conflicts, succession disputes, and shifting allegiances as ambitious princes vied for supremacy.

Despite the political turbulence, the Karakhanid era was a period of immense cultural significance. While they embraced the high culture of the cities they conquered and continued to use Persian for many administrative purposes, they also elevated their own native Turkic language to a language of literature and court. For the first time, a Turkic dialect, written in the Arabic script, was used to produce major literary and scholarly works within the urban heart of Central Asia. The most important of these was the

Kutadgu Bilig ("The Wisdom of Royal Glory"), composed in 1069 by Yusuf Khass Hajib of Balasagun. An epic poem of political and ethical advice for rulers, it is a foundational text of Turkic literature, blending Islamic principles of justice with ancient Turkic traditions of statecraft. Another seminal work from this period is the *Dīwān Lughāt al-Turk* ("Compendium of the Turkic Dialects"), written by Mahmud al-Kashgari. It was an encyclopedic dictionary intended to teach the Arabic-speaking caliphs about the richness of the Turkic language and culture, a clear sign of growing Turkic pride and influence.

The Karakhanids were also prolific builders. They adorned their cities, particularly Bukhara and Samarkand, with mosques, madrasas, and mausoleums. One of their most enduring monuments is the Kalyan Minaret in Bukhara. Completed in 1127, this towering structure of baked brick soars nearly 47 meters into the sky. Its intricate brickwork patterns are a testament to the skill of the era's architects, and it was so impressive that even Genghis Khan, who leveled most of the city, is said to have spared it. The Karakhanids presided over a period of economic prosperity, minting their own coins and overseeing the continued flourishing of the Silk Road trade. Their rule cemented the political and demographic dominance of Turkic peoples in Mawarannahr, accelerating the linguistic shift from Iranian languages to Turkic in many rural areas, a process that would shape the ethnolinguistic identity of modern Uzbekistan.

While the Karakhanids were consolidating their rule north of the Amu Darya, the lands to the south fell to a dynasty with very different origins. The Ghaznavids emerged not from the steppe, but from the very heart of the Samanid military machine. The dynasty was founded by Alptigin, a Turkic slave-general in the Samanid army who, after falling out of favor at court, used his personal troops to seize the remote mountain fortress of Ghazna in modern Afghanistan in 962. He ruled this small domain as a local lord, as did his successor and son-in-law, Sabuktigin, another former slave. Sabuktigin expanded his territory and, while still paying nominal allegiance to the Samanids, operated as an independent king in all but name. The true architect of the

Ghaznavid Empire, however, was his son, a man whose name would echo through history as a byword for both fabulous wealth and ruthless conquest: Mahmud of Ghazni.

Casting off the last pretense of Samanid authority in 998, Mahmud secured an agreement with the Karakhanids to partition the dying state. He took control of Khurasan and all the lands south of the Amu Darya, while the Karakhanids held Mawarannahr. Mahmud was a military genius, and he spent the majority of his thirty-two-year reign on campaign. His primary target was the vast and disunited Indian subcontinent. He launched seventeen devastating raids into northern India, smashing the armies of Hindu princes, plundering the unimaginable wealth of temples, and carrying back to Ghazna a fortune in gold, silver, gems, and slaves. These campaigns were justified in the language of holy war, and Mahmud cultivated the image of himself as a peerless champion of Sunni Islam. The Abbasid Caliph in Baghdad, powerless to stop him but eager to claim a successful commander as his own, showered him with titles, most famously *Yamin al-Dawla*, "the Right Hand of the State."

This Indian wealth funded the creation of a vast and powerful empire. Unlike the decentralized Karakhanid state, the Ghaznavid Empire was a highly centralized autocracy, modeled directly on Samanid and Abbasid administrative principles. The court, the bureaucracy, and the culture were thoroughly Persianized. The language of government and poetry was Persian, and Mahmud's administration was run by sophisticated Persian viziers. He used his immense riches to transform his capital, Ghazna, from a mountain backwater into a magnificent imperial city, a center of art, architecture, and learning that was said to rival Baghdad. He built a grand mosque, the "Celestial Bride," along with lavish palaces, libraries, and gardens. He was a master of propaganda, understanding that cultural splendor was as important as military might in projecting power.

Mahmud's court became a magnet for some of the greatest minds of the age, drawing in scholars and poets with the promise of lavish patronage, whether they wanted to come or not. When

Mahmud conquered the autonomous kingdom of Khwarazm in 1017, he brought its leading intellectuals back to his capital, including the brilliant polymath Abu Rayhan al-Biruni. Though Biruni was essentially a well-treated hostage, he used his time to conduct groundbreaking studies of Indian culture, science, and religion. It was also at Mahmud's court that the poet Ferdowsi hoped to find a patron for his monumental epic, the *Shahnameh* ("The Book of Kings"), the definitive account of Iran's pre-Islamic history. The story of their interaction is legendary; Mahmud, a pragmatic Turkic warrior, was reportedly unimpressed with the tales of ancient Persian heroes and failed to pay the poet the promised price, a slight that earned the sultan an immortal place in Ferdowsi's satirical verses.

For several decades, the two Turkic empires coexisted, with the Amu Darya serving as a largely respected, though occasionally contested, frontier. Their relationship was a mixture of rivalry and grudging respect, punctuated by occasional treaties, marriage alliances, and conflicts. Together, they represented the new political synthesis of the region: Turkic military elites ruling over a predominantly Persian-speaking urban and agricultural population, within the established framework of Islamic civilization. The Ghaznavids embodied the more autocratic, Persianized model of this synthesis, while the Karakhanids represented a looser, more tribally-oriented version that gave greater prominence to Turkic cultural traditions.

The glory of both dynasties, however, was not destined to last. The Ghaznavid Empire's reliance on plunder from India was unsustainable, and its power was brittle. The greatest threat came not from the Karakhanids but from another group of Turks, the Seljuks, who had been allowed to settle in Khurasan. Under their leaders Tughril and Chaghri Beg, the Seljuks rose in rebellion against Mahmud's less capable son, Mas'ud. In 1040, at the Battle of Dandanaqan near Merv, the Seljuk cavalry decisively crushed the larger Ghaznavid army. This single defeat was a catastrophe from which the Ghaznavids never recovered. They lost Khurasan and all their western territories permanently, retreating to their core domains in eastern Afghanistan and northern India, where they survived as a diminished local power for another 150 years.

The Karakhanids, meanwhile, endured for longer, but their inherent political disunity made them vulnerable. The victorious Seljuks swept over the Amu Darya and for a time turned the western Karakhanid khans into their vassals. Though they would later regain a measure of independence, the Karakhanid state remained fractured and weakened by its endless internal power struggles. By the twelfth century, they were caught between the pressure of new nomadic groups from the east, like the Qara Khitai, and the rising power of a new dynasty from within the region, the Khwarazmshahs. The era of the first Turkic empires was drawing to a close, but their legacy was profound. They had definitively shifted the political center of gravity in Central Asia into Turkic hands and established the enduring synthesis of Turkic rule and Perso-Islamic culture that would define the region for centuries to come.

CHAPTER EIGHT: The Khwarazmian Empire and its Dominion

The eleventh and twelfth centuries had redrawn the map of Central Asia. The great Seljuk Empire, a Turkic dynasty that had swept out of the steppes to conquer everything from the Amu Darya to the Mediterranean, was now a shadow of its former self. After the death of the formidable Sultan Sanjar in 1157, the empire had crumbled into a patchwork of successor states, each ruled by an ambitious general or a rival branch of the Seljuk family. The once-unquestioned authority that had imposed a semblance of order over the eastern Islamic world was gone. This fragmentation created a power vacuum, a political void into which a new, aggressive, and ultimately tragic empire would rise. Its heartland was one of the region's most ancient and distinctive oases: Khwarazm.

Nestled in the fertile delta of the Amu Darya south of the Aral Sea, Khwarazm had always been a world apart. Its relative isolation, ancient Iranian heritage, and unique culture had given its people a fierce sense of independence. The title of its ruler, the Khwarazmshah, was an ancient one, stretching back into the pre-Islamic past. The dynasty that would carry this title to its greatest heights, however, was of more recent and humbler stock. Its story began not with an ancient king, but with a Turkic slave named Anushtegin Gharchai. Anushtegin was a cupbearer in the court of the great Seljuk Sultan Malik-Shah, a position of trust that gave him proximity to power. In recognition of his service, around 1077, the Sultan appointed him governor of Khwarazm.

This was a standard administrative appointment, but it planted the seed of a future dynasty. Anushtegin's son, Qutb al-Din Muhammad, inherited the post in 1097 and, through shrewd management and unwavering loyalty to the Seljuk Sultan Sanjar, managed to make the governorship a hereditary possession of his family. For the first time, this new line of Khwarazmshahs had put down permanent roots. They were, however, model vassals, dutifully paying their tribute to the Seljuk court and acknowledging Sanjar as their supreme overlord. This phase of quiet consolidation changed dramatically with the accession of Qutb al-Din's son, Ala al-Din Atsiz, in 1127.

Atsiz was a man of boundless ambition and cunning, a master of the political tightrope walk. While openly proclaiming his loyalty to Sultan Sanjar, he spent his entire reign subtly and not-so-subtly undermining Seljuk authority and expanding his own. He was a quintessential opportunist, sensing the growing weakness at the heart of the great empire. His first moves were to secure his immediate frontiers. He launched successful campaigns north into the vast Kipchak steppe, subduing the nomadic tribes and, crucially, incorporating their formidable cavalrymen into his own army. This gave him a powerful military force that was independent of Seljuk control.

His relationship with Sultan Sanjar was a masterclass in calculated insubordination. He would rebel, get defeated, beg for forgiveness, be reinstated, and then immediately begin plotting his next move. At one point, Sanjar, exasperated by his vassal's constant scheming, invaded Khwarazm and forced Atsiz to flee. Yet, the Sultan always found it more practical to have the capable Atsiz ruling the remote province than to try and govern it directly. This decades-long dance of rebellion and reconciliation allowed Atsiz to methodically build a powerful, semi-independent state under the very nose of his overlord. The decisive break he had been waiting for came not from his own actions, but from a cataclysmic event on the Seljuks' eastern border.

In 1141, a new power that had migrated from northern China, the Qara Khitai, engaged the Seljuk army at the Battle of Qatwan, in the plains near Samarkand. The Qara Khitai were not Muslims, and their arrival sent shockwaves through the Islamic world. The battle was an unmitigated disaster for the Seljuks. Sultan Sanjar's seemingly invincible army was utterly crushed, his power and prestige shattered in a single afternoon. Atsiz, ever the opportunist, immediately seized the advantage. He swept into the great Khurasanian cities of Merv and Nishapur, looting the Seljuk treasuries and temporarily adding the province to his domain. He had thrown off one master, but in doing so, he had inadvertently acquired another. The victorious Qara Khitai were now the dominant power in the region, and they promptly made the Khwarazmshahs their vassals, forcing Atsiz to pay them a hefty annual tribute. For the next seventy years, the primary goal of Khwarazmian foreign policy would be to rid themselves of this humiliating and expensive overlordship.

Atsiz's successors, Il-Arslan and Ala al-Din Tekish, continued his policies, patiently expanding their territory while chafing under Qara Khitai suzerainty. It was Tekish who transformed Khwarazm from a regional power into a true empire. A ruthless and capable ruler, he spent his reign consolidating his control over Khurasan and systematically dismantling the last vestiges of Seljuk power in Persia. His crowning achievement came in 1194 when he met and defeated the army of the last Seljuk Sultan of Iran, Tughril III. The Sultan was killed in the battle, and his head was sent to the Abbasid Caliph in Baghdad as a grisly trophy. With this victory, the Seljuk Empire was formally extinguished, and the Khwarazmshah Tekish stood as the most powerful monarch in the eastern Islamic world.

This rapid rise to prominence created a new and dangerous rivalry. In Baghdad, the Abbasid Caliph al-Nasir, a politically astute and ambitious pontiff, saw the new Khwarazmian empire not as a protector but as a direct threat to his own authority. He viewed the Khwarazmshahs as uncouth Turkic upstarts and worked tirelessly behind the scenes to undermine their power, intriguing with their enemies and refusing to grant them the formal recognition they craved. This mutual suspicion and hostility between the Caliph and the Shah would become a festering wound in the heart of the Islamic east.

The empire reached its zenith under Tekish's son, Ala al-Din Muhammad II, who ascended the throne in 1200. Muhammad II was consumed by a desire for glory, seeing himself as a new Alexander the Great, destined for world conquest. His early reign was marked by a series of stunning military successes. He completed the conquest of Persia, subdued the Ghurid dynasty in Afghanistan, and pushed his borders to the edge of India. His greatest triumph came around 1210 when he finally confronted and destroyed the power of his family's long-time overlords, the Qara Khitai. This victory was celebrated across the Muslim world. Muhammad II had not only liberated his realm from a non-Muslim power but had also extinguished it, a feat that earned him immense prestige. He was now, in his own mind, the undisputed champion of Islam.

By 1217, the Khwarazmian Empire was a colossal entity, one of the largest in the world. It stretched from the Syr Darya river in the north to the Persian Gulf in the south, from the Indus River to the Zagros Mountains. The great cities of the Silk Road—Samarkand, Bukhara, Nishapur, Merv, and the Khwarazmian capital of Gurganj—were all under his command. To reflect his new imperial status, Muhammad II moved his capital from Gurganj to the ancient and glorious city of Samarkand, transforming it into the center of his vast domain. He adopted the title "Sultan" and demanded that the Abbasid Caliph in Baghdad recognize him as the supreme temporal ruler of the entire Islamic east. When the Caliph inevitably refused, Muhammad II took a fateful step. He had his own religious scholars declare the Caliph deposed and proclaimed a rival Caliph of his own choosing. He then assembled an army to march on Baghdad itself, an act of supreme arrogance aimed at humbling the spiritual head of Sunni Islam. The campaign was a fiasco, getting bogged down by an early winter in the mountains of Persia, but the message was clear: Muhammad II answered to no one.

On paper, the empire was invincible, a military superpower with a vast population and immense wealth. In reality, it was a fragile construct, a house of cards built on shaky foundations. Its rapid conquest had created a host of internal problems that its arrogant ruler chose to ignore. The most serious of these problems lived in his own palace: his mother, Terken Khatun. A woman of forceful personality and political skill, Terken Khatun was from the powerful Qangli Turkic tribe, the same tribe from which the Khwarazmian army drew most of its elite soldiers. Her power was immense and independent of her son's. She maintained her own court at the old capital of Gurganj, controlled the state treasury, and appointed her relatives to the highest military commands. She frequently countermanded the Sultan's orders and protected her favorites from his wrath. This created a disastrous division of authority at the very top of the empire, with two rival power centers constantly working at cross-purposes.

The army itself was another critical weakness. It was a massive force, composed largely of Turkic mercenaries, primarily the Qangli and Kipchak kinsmen of Terken Khatun. These soldiers were loyal not to the Sultan or the state, but to their own commanders and, by extension, to the queen mother. While effective on the battlefield, they were notoriously undisciplined off it. They treated the empire's Persian-speaking urban and agricultural population with contempt, plundering the countryside and alienating the very people whose taxes supported the state. Resentment against the brutal Turkic soldiery simmered throughout the empire, ensuring that the Sultan ruled over a population that feared, but did not love, him.

Furthermore, the empire was not a unified state but a collection of recently conquered territories held together by military force alone. Muhammad II had not had the time or the inclination to build a stable, unified administration. He ruled by terror and intimidation, alienating local dynasties and executing anyone he suspected of disloyalty. His own personality exacerbated these problems. He was notoriously suspicious, volatile, and indecisive. He trusted no one, not even his own sons, whom he appointed to governorships but stripped of any real power. Centralizing all decision-making in his own hands, he created an administrative bottleneck that left the empire dangerously unresponsive.

It was in this climate of supreme overconfidence and deep-seated internal rot that the first whispers of a new power were heard from the far east. Muhammad II, busy with his grand project of conquering the world and quarreling with the Caliph, paid little attention to reports of a new Mongol khan named Genghis who was unifying the tribes of the steppe. The Khwarazmian sphere of influence now bordered this new confederation, and commercial contacts began. In 1218, a large caravan of several hundred merchants, sent by the Mongol ruler to establish trade relations, arrived at the Khwarazmian frontier city of Otrar on the Syr Darya.

The governor of Otrar was a man named Inalchuq, a relative of the powerful Terken Khatun. Coveting the rich goods in the caravan and deeply suspicious of the merchants' intentions, he accused them of being Mongol spies. He arrested the entire party and sent a message to Sultan Muhammad II in Samarkand, seeking permission to execute them. In a decision that would seal the fate of millions, the Sultan, without any serious investigation and perhaps swayed by Inalchuq's greed or his own arrogance, gave his consent. The merchants were all put to the sword, and their goods were seized.

Genghis Khan, adhering to the strict diplomatic protocols of the steppe, dispatched a second mission, a delegation of three envoys, to demand that the governor of Otrar be handed over for punishment and the confiscated goods returned. The response of Sultan Muhammad II was one of catastrophic and inexplicable folly. In a final, fatal act of defiance, he had the chief Mongol envoy executed and the other two publicly humiliated by having their beards shaved off before sending them back. There could be no greater insult, no clearer declaration of war. In the vast grasslands to the east, the master of the Mongol hordes received the news. The die was cast. The storm was about to break.

CHAPTER NINE: The Mongol Invasion and its Aftermath

The message delivered by the two shaven-headed envoys was not just an insult; it was a death warrant. For Genghis Khan, the master of the Mongol steppe, the execution of his ambassadors and the murder of his merchants at Otrar was a violation of the most sacred laws of nations, an act of perfidy that demanded retribution on a scale the world had never witnessed. This was no longer a matter of trade disputes or border skirmishes. The actions of Sultan Muhammad II had made it a matter of honor and a question of cosmic justice. The Sultan, in his arrogance, had awakened a storm, and now the wind was set to blow from the east with unimaginable fury.

Throughout 1219, the Mongol war machine, the most disciplined and mobile military force on the planet, prepared for the invasion. This was not to be a simple punitive raid but a full-scale war of annihilation. Genghis Khan summoned his sons, his generals, and the warriors of all the tribes he had unified. An army of well over one hundred thousand men was assembled, each man a hardened veteran of steppe warfare, an expert horseman and archer. This was an army that traveled light, sustained itself on the move, and was bound by an iron discipline unknown in the fractious, mercenary-heavy forces of the Khwarazmian Empire. They possessed a sophisticated system of intelligence gathering, a mastery of siegecraft learned from captured Chinese engineers, and a command structure that allowed for complex, coordinated movements across vast distances.

Sultan Muhammad II, for his part, seemed paralyzed by the very crisis he had created. Despite commanding a numerically superior army, he was plagued by indecision and suspicion. He distrusted his own commanders, particularly the relatives of his powerful mother, Terken Khatun, fearing that a unified army might be turned against him in a coup. Instead of concentrating his forces to meet the Mongols in a decisive battle, he made the catastrophic decision to disperse his troops, garrisoning them in the major cities across his empire. His strategy was to turn his realm into a giant sieve, hoping the Mongols would exhaust themselves in a series of difficult sieges, allowing him to pick them off later. He had fatally underestimated his opponent's grasp of strategy and their capacity for relentless, systematic destruction.

In the autumn of 1219, the Mongol host descended upon Mawarannahr. This was not a single, lumbering column but a sophisticated multi-pronged assault designed to confuse and overwhelm. One Mongol army under Genghis Khan's sons Chagatai and Ogedei marched directly to the frontier city of Otrar to begin the grim work of retribution. Another column under his eldest son, Jochi, moved north to strike at the cities along the Syr Darya. The Sultan, expecting a frontal assault along these conventional routes, waited with his main army near Samarkand. He failed to account for the strategic audacity of Genghis Khan himself.

While his sons pinned down the Khwarazmian frontier forces, Genghis Khan took the main body of his army and vanished. Accompanied by his brilliant general Subutai, he led his warriors on one of the most daring flanking maneuvers in military history. He turned south, into the seemingly impassable Kyzylkum desert, a vast and waterless expanse of red sand. For weeks, guided by captured nomads, the Mongol army traversed the desert, emerging as if from nowhere in the heart of the Khwarazmian empire, deep behind enemy lines. In February 1220, the garrison and citizens of Bukhara awoke to find not a raiding party, but the main Mongol army, with the Great Khan at its head, encamped before their walls.

The shock and terror were absolute. The Sultan's entire defensive strategy had been rendered irrelevant in a single stroke. The Turkic garrison in Bukhara attempted a sortie but was quickly annihilated by the Mongol vanguard. Seeing the hopelessness of their situation, the city's civilian leaders, composed of merchants and clergy, opened the gates and surrendered, hoping for mercy. Genghis Khan rode his horse into the courtyard of the city's main

Friday mosque. In a scene that would be retold for centuries, he is said to have had the sacred chests containing the Qur'an brought out to be used as mangers for his horses while he ascended the pulpit and declared himself to be the "flail of God," sent to punish them for their sins.

The city's citadel, holding a few thousand loyalist soldiers, held out for a few more days, but its resistance only sealed Bukhara's fate. Once the citadel was taken, the Mongol retribution was unleashed. The garrison was massacred to a man. The city was systematically plundered. Young men were conscripted into labor battalions to be used as human shields in future sieges, while women and skilled artisans were enslaved and divided up among the Mongol conquerors. Then, the city was set ablaze. The fires raged for days, destroying much of the city, which was largely built of wood, save for the great Kalyan Minaret and a few other brick structures that survived the inferno. Noble Bukhara, the Dome of Islam, had been reduced to a smoldering ruin in less than two weeks.

Leaving a trail of devastation behind him, Genghis Khan moved on to the ultimate prize: the imperial capital of Samarkand. News of Bukhara's fate had preceded him, sowing terror and despair. Samarkand was a far more formidable objective. It was protected by massive walls, reputedly defended by a garrison of over one hundred thousand men, and even equipped with a number of war elephants. But the city was crippled by the same internal divisions that plagued the empire. The Turkic garrison was at odds with the Persian-speaking citizenry, and the arrival of the Mongol army brought these tensions to a boiling point.

The siege was brutally efficient. Genghis Khan used the thousands of captives herded from Bukhara as a human screen, forcing them to fill the city's moat and undermine its walls. After a few days of intense fighting and a failed counter-attack by the garrison, morale within the city collapsed. A delegation of citizens, desperate to avoid the fate of Bukhara, secretly negotiated a surrender with the Mongols, opening the gates to them in March 1220. As before, the citadel garrison fought on and was duly exterminated. The city was then subjected to the same dreadful process. A wholesale massacre took place, with Persian chroniclers claiming that a million people were killed, a number that, while likely an exaggeration, speaks to the immense scale of the slaughter. Tens of thousands of the city's famed craftsmen and artisans were spared, only to be enslaved and sent back to Mongolia to serve their new masters. The magnificent capital of the Khwarazmian Empire, a city of turquoise domes and bustling markets, was gutted and silenced.

While his empire crumbled, Sultan Muhammad II proved to be a leader utterly devoid of courage. Instead of rallying his remaining armies or organizing a defense, he simply fled. As the Mongols took Samarkand, he was already on the run westward, abandoning his people and his throne. Genghis Khan dispatched two of his finest generals, the legendary commanders Jebe and Subutai, with twenty thousand horsemen and a simple order: hunt down the Shah and do not return until he is captured, dead or alive. What followed was an epic pursuit across half a continent. Jebe and Subutai chased the disgraced Sultan through Persia, destroying any city that offered him aid. The Shah fled from Nishapur to Rayy to Hamadan, his authority evaporating with every mile. Finally, broken and abandoned by his last followers, he took refuge on a small, barren island in the Caspian Sea, where he died of pleurisy in the winter of 1220, a destitute fugitive on the edge of his own stolen empire.

With the Sultan dead and the great cities of Mawarannahr in ruins, the Mongol armies turned their attention to the empire's heartland, Khwarazm itself. In 1221, a large Mongol force under the command of Genghis Khan's three sons—Jochi, Chagatai, and Ogedei—laid siege to the old capital, Gurganj (modern-day Urgench). This was a city that would not go quietly. It was the home turf of the powerful Qangli Turkic elite loyal to Terken Khatun, and its defenders mounted a resistance of legendary ferocity.

The siege of Gurganj was the longest and bloodiest of the entire campaign. The flat, marshy terrain of the delta made it difficult for the Mongols to employ their usual tactics. The city's defenders fought for every street, every house. The siege dragged on for months, costing the Mongols heavy casualties and fraying the tempers of the three brothers, who quarreled bitterly over strategy. When the city's outer walls were finally breached, the fighting descended into a horrific, close-quarter battle through the streets. The Mongols were forced to take the city block by block, burning down sections with naphtha and slaughtering the inhabitants as they went. After the last pocket of resistance was crushed, the victors took their revenge. The surviving population was herded out onto the plains, where the usual division took place: artisans and young women were enslaved, and the rest were systematically executed. To complete the city's destruction and render it uninhabitable forever, the Mongols broke the dikes on the Amu Darya, diverting the river's course to flood the ruins entirely. Gurganj, one of the greatest and most vibrant cities in Central Asia, was literally wiped from the face of the earth.

Not all was cowardice and collapse. Amidst the ashes of his father's empire, a figure of heroic resistance emerged: Muhammad's eldest son, Jalal al-Din Mangburni. Unlike his father, Jalal al-Din was a warrior of immense personal bravery and considerable tactical skill. Fleeing south into the region of modern Afghanistan, he managed to gather the remnants of the Khwarazmian armies and rally a new force around him. He proved to be a formidable opponent. In the spring of 1221, near the town of Parwan, north of Kabul, Jalal al-Din's army confronted a Mongol division. In a carefully planned battle, he lured the Mongols into a narrow valley and inflicted a rare and shocking defeat upon them, one of the few setbacks they would suffer in the entire war.

The news of this victory sparked premature uprisings in several of the conquered cities, which were brutally suppressed. Genghis Khan, who had been consolidating his rule in Samarkand, could not tolerate such an act of defiance. He took personal command of an army and marched south to hunt down the upstart prince. He cornered Jalal al-Din and his much smaller force on the banks of the Indus River. In a desperate battle, Jalal al-Din's army was overwhelmed. Seeing all was lost, the prince mounted his horse and, in a final act of legendary defiance, spurred it over the cliff edge, plunging into the turbulent waters of the Indus and successfully swimming to the other side. Genghis Khan, watching from the cliff, is said to have forbidden his archers to shoot, expressing admiration for the courage of his enemy. Though Jalal al-Din would spend the next decade as a wandering adventurer fighting in India and the Caucasus, his resistance in the east was over.

By 1223, the Mongol conquest of Mawarannahr and Khurasan was complete. The wave of destruction had passed, leaving behind a landscape of utter desolation. The devastation was on a scale that is difficult to comprehend. The great cities that had been the jewels of the Islamic east were now depopulated ruins. Chroniclers of the time wrote of a land where one could travel for days without hearing the crow of a rooster or the bark of a dog. The human cost was staggering, with death tolls certainly running into the millions.

The long-term damage went even deeper than the urban slaughter. For millennia, the prosperity of the region had depended on its vast and intricate network of irrigation canals, which diverted water from the Amu Darya and Syr Darya to turn the arid plains into fertile fields. In their destructive fury, the Mongols systematically destroyed this vital infrastructure. Canals were broken, dikes were leveled, and the qanats—the underground water channels—were filled in. The result was catastrophic. Vast swathes of cultivated land reverted to desert, a process of ecological devastation from which some parts of the region would never fully recover. The sedentary, agricultural basis of society was shattered.

The old political and social order was completely obliterated. The Khwarazmian state, the local Iranian *dihqan* aristocracy that had survived for centuries, and the urban merchant class were all gone, either killed, enslaved, or scattered. Into this vacuum stepped the new Mongol military administration. Genghis Khan appointed governors, known as *darughachi* or *baskaks*, to oversee the ruined territories. Their primary job was simple: to count the survivors, organize them into taxable units, and begin extracting whatever wealth remained for the benefit of the Mongol Empire. A new census was conducted, and a harsh tax regime was imposed. The survivors were put to work rebuilding strategic infrastructure, but the glory of the past was gone. Mawarannahr had been transformed from a vibrant, world-leading center of civilization into a battered and impoverished province of a vast, steppe-based empire, whose new masters were far away and had little understanding of, or concern for, the urban and agricultural world they now ruled.

CHAPTER TEN: The Chagatai Khanate and the Rise of Turco-Mongol Traditions

When the Flail of God, Genghis Khan, died in 1227 while on campaign in China, he left behind him a world remade by the sword and an empire that stretched from the Pacific Ocean to the Caspian Sea. An empire of this magnitude, held together by the will of a single, extraordinary man, could not survive its founder intact. Following Mongol tradition, the vast dominion was apportioned among his four sons by his chief wife, Börte. The eldest, Jochi, who had predeceased his father, had his inheritance in the western steppes passed to his own sons, who would found the Golden Horde. The third son, Ogedei, was designated as the new Great Khan, ruling from the Mongol heartland of Karakorum. The youngest, Tolui, served as regent and inherited the Mongolian homeland itself. The second son, a man known for his stern and unyielding nature, was Chagatai, and his inheritance, his *ulus*, comprised the heart of Central Asia. It was a poisoned chalice of ruined cities, depopulated farmlands, and a traumatized population, and it would bear his name for centuries to come: the Chagatai Khanate.

Chagatai Khan was, by all accounts, his father's son in temperament, if not in strategic genius. He was a conservative, a traditionalist, and above all, the self-appointed guardian of the Great *Yasa*, the secret code of Mongol laws and customs established by Genghis Khan. The *Yasa* was more than a legal framework; it was the embodiment of the Mongol way of life, a code for warriors of the high steppe. It dictated everything from military discipline to the proper way to butcher an animal. For Chagatai, the *Yasa* was absolute, and its enforcement was his primary duty. This zealous adherence to Mongol tradition immediately created a deep and irreconcilable conflict with the culture of the people he now ruled. Mawarannahr was a land steeped in a millennium of Islamic law and Persian urbanity, and its customs were in direct opposition to the Mongol code.

The points of friction were numerous and profound. Islamic Sharia required that an animal's throat be cut and its blood drained for the meat to be considered *halal*, or permissible. The *Yasa*, on the other hand, strictly forbade the spilling of blood onto the earth, mandating that the animal's heart be seized or its spine broken. Islamic law prescribed ritual ablutions with running water before prayer; the *Yasa* forbade bathing in rivers during the summer, believing it would provoke the sky-spirits and cause thunderstorms. For the settled, Muslim population, these were matters of profound religious importance. For Chagatai and his Mongol elite, they were flagrant violations of the sacred law of their ancestors. Chagatai's reign was therefore not one of reconciliation, but of imposition. He established his court, his *ordu*, not in the ruins of Samarkand or Bukhara, but in the traditional nomadic fashion, moving with the seasons through the grasslands of the Ili River valley, east of Lake Balkhash. From this remote steppe headquarters, he governed his settled subjects with a detached and often brutal hand.

While the Khan and his Mongol warriors concerned themselves with the *Yasa* and the administration of the military, the practical task of governing a ruined civilization fell to a class of skilled administrators who were not Mongols. The Great Khan Ogedei, recognizing that a land of terrified peasants and dead merchants could produce no tax revenue, appointed a remarkable man named Mahmud Yalavach to oversee the civil administration of the entire region. Mahmud, believed to have been a Khwarazmian merchant, understood that the only way to extract wealth was to first create it. He and, more importantly, his son and successor Mas'ud Beg, became the architects of a slow and painful recovery. They were the indispensable middlemen, bridging the vast cultural gap between the nomadic conquerors and the settled conquered.

Mas'ud Beg, who administered Mawarannahr for a remarkable fifty years until his death in 1289, serving a succession of Khans, implemented a series of crucial reforms. He reorganized the tax system, replacing arbitrary plunder with a predictable, fixed levy on agriculture and commerce. He understood that cities were the engines of the economy, and he worked to repopulate them, offering incentives for artisans and merchants to return and rebuild their shattered lives. Under his careful stewardship, the slow pulse of urban life began to return to Bukhara and Samarkand. The bazaars reopened, the craft workshops were re-established, and caravans once again began to tentatively ply the ancient trade routes. This created a peculiar dual system of government. In the cities and fields, the Persian-speaking bureaucracy of Mas'ud Beg held sway, collecting taxes and administering civil justice. But looming over them was the ever-present authority of the Mongol military elite, the true masters of the land, who enforced the *Yasa* and were interested only in the steady flow of revenue from the subjects Mas'ud managed.

This uneasy coexistence was mirrored by a slow, creeping transformation within the ruling Mongol elite itself. They had arrived as a small, alien aristocracy in a sea of Turkic and Persian-speaking peoples. While the first generation, men like Chagatai, held fast to their language and customs, their descendants could not remain immune to the culture of the world they now inhabited. The most significant change was linguistic. The majority population of the region, especially in the countryside, had been Turkic-speaking for centuries. Over generations, the Mongol rulers and their followers began to abandon their own Mongol tongue in favor of the local Turkic dialect. This emerging language, heavily influenced by Persian and Arabic but built on a Karluk Turkic grammatical base, became known as Chagatai Turkic. It was the language of the new, hybrid ruling class and would eventually become a major literary language, the ancestor of modern Uzbek.

The more contentious transformation was religious. While the Mongol elite was slowly becoming Turkified in speech, it remained deeply divided over the question of Islam. The fundamental conflict that had defined Chagatai's reign, between the nomadic, shamanist traditions of the *Yasa* and the settled, urban world of Sharia, became the central political fault line of the Khanate for the next century. This was not merely a theological debate; it was a clash of civilizations played out within a single ruling family. One faction, the traditionalists, advocated for maintaining the pure Mongol way of life. They were contemptuous of cities, which they saw as corrupting, and viewed Islam as a threat to their identity. Their power base was in the eastern, steppe regions of the Khanate, which they called Moghulistan, the "Land of the Mongols."

The other faction was composed of those princes and nobles who saw their future in collaboration with their subjects. They recognized the administrative and cultural power of Islam and were drawn to the wealth and sophistication of the great cities. They understood that to effectively rule Mawarannahr, it was better to adopt the faith of its people. This faction's strength lay in the west, in the rebuilt oases of Bukhara and Samarkand. The history of the Chagatai Khanate throughout the late thirteenth and early fourteenth centuries is a dizzying succession of coups and counter-coups, as khans from one faction were enthroned and then violently deposed by the other. In 1266, a Chagataid prince named Mubarak Shah became the first of his line to convert to Islam, a landmark moment that proved to be short-lived. He was overthrown within months by his cousin, who represented the traditionalist faction.

The tide began to turn decisively in favor of the settled faction under the rule of Kebek Khan, who reigned from 1318 to 1326. Kebek was a pragmatist and a reformer. He broke with the nomadic tradition of shunning cities and established a fixed capital for the first time. In the fertile valley of the Kashka Darya, near the ancient city of Nakhshab, he built a grand palace, a *qarshi* in the Mongol tongue. This settlement grew into the modern city of Qarshi, a monument to his reign. Kebek also introduced a unified and standardized coinage, stamped with his name, which replaced the chaotic mix of currencies that had previously hindered trade. He actively encouraged the rebuilding of agriculture and commerce, recognizing that his own power and wealth depended on the prosperity of his subjects. While not a Muslim himself, his policies created an environment where the Perso-Islamic urban culture could recover and thrive.

Kebek's reforms, however, provoked a fierce backlash from the Moghulistan traditionalists, who saw his embrace of urban life as a betrayal of the Mongol way. The conflict came to a head under his brother, Tarmashirin, who came to the throne in 1331. Tarmashirin went a step further than Kebek: he converted to Islam and attempted to make it the state religion, reportedly demanding that his Mongol nobles follow his example. For the eastern chieftains, this was the final straw. Proclaiming that Tarmashirin had abandoned the Great *Yasa*, they rose in rebellion, marched west, and overthrew and killed him in 1334.

The execution of Tarmashirin marked the point of no return. The Chagatai Khanate, which had long been a state with two competing identities, now shattered into two distinct geographical and cultural entities. In the east, in Moghulistan, a new line of khans from the house of Chagatai re-established a purely nomadic, traditionalist Mongol state. They would remain a powerful force on the steppes for centuries, frequently launching raids into the settled lands to their west.

In the west, in Mawarannahr, the authority of the khan collapsed completely. The great Turco-Mongol tribal leaders, the *amirs*, seized real power. The Chagatai khans who were placed on the throne after Tarmashirin were nothing more than powerless puppets, legitimizing figureheads whose Chinggisid lineage provided a necessary illusion of continuity. The real rulers were the amirs of powerful clans like the Barlas, the Jalayir, the Süldüs, and the Arlat. These men were the ultimate product of the century-long synthesis: Mongol by ancestry, Turkic by language, often Muslim by faith, and fiercely competitive by nature. The once-great *ulus* of Chagatai devolved into a chaotic patchwork of competing tribal territories, a state of endemic civil war where amirs made and unmade khans at will and constantly battled one another for supremacy. It was a world of shifting alliances and brutal betrayals, a political landscape where only the most ruthless and ambitious could survive. It was into this crucible of Turco-Mongol anarchy that a young nobleman from the Barlas tribe, born just two years after the murder of Tarmashirin, would take his first steps. His name was Timur.

CHAPTER ELEVEN: Amir Timur and the Timurid Empire: A Central Asian Renaissance

The world into which Timur was born in 1336 was a fractured and dangerous one. The great *ulus* of Chagatai was a khanate in name only, its authority shattered. Mawarannahr had devolved into a lawless arena for the ambitions of rival Turco-Mongol chieftains. These amirs, leaders of powerful tribes like the Barlas, Jalayir, and Qara'unas, paid lip service to a succession of puppet khans, but in reality, they were kings in their own right, carving out petty domains and waging a relentless, low-grade war against one another. It was a landscape of shifting loyalties, casual betrayal, and brutal, small-scale conflict. For a young man of noble birth, boundless ambition, and a conspicuous lack of scruples, it was a world of immense opportunity.

Timur, born into the Barlas clan in the green valley surrounding the city of Kesh, the future Shahrisabz, was a product of this environment. He was not a prince destined for a throne but a minor aristocrat who would have to seize his own destiny. His early life was the stuff of adventure and brigandage. He was a cattle rustler, a mercenary captain, and a leader of a small gang of sworn followers, honing his skills in leadership and desert warfare in the harsh school of the Central Asian plains. It was during one of these early skirmishes that he sustained two severe wounds to his right leg and right hand, leaving him with a permanent limp and a partially paralyzed arm. This injury earned him the Persian nickname that would follow him into history: *Timur-i-Leng*, or Timur the Lame, a name later Europeanized into the formidable-sounding Tamerlane.

His rise from minor chieftain to regional contender was a masterclass in political maneuvering. He possessed an uncanny ability to read the motivations of others and to forge and break alliances with perfect, ruthless timing. His first significant partnership was with his brother-in-law, Amir Husayn of the Qara'unas tribe, a grandson of the last effective ruler of the unified Chagatai Khanate. Together, they presented a united front against the depredations of the Moghul khans from the east, who sought to re-impose their authority over the rich cities of Mawarannahr. For years, Timur and Husayn were inseparable partners, at times victorious, at others hunted fugitives, their fortunes rising and falling with the tide of war.

This partnership, born of necessity, could not survive the strain of their competing ambitions. As their power grew, so did their suspicion of one another. Husayn, as the more senior and powerful of the two, saw Timur as a useful but subordinate ally. Timur, possessed of a far greater strategic and military genius, saw Husayn as an obstacle. The final break came in 1370. After a series of disagreements, Timur marshaled his forces and laid siege to Husayn in his stronghold of Balkh. The city fell, and Husayn, after a brief attempt to hide, was captured and conveniently killed by one of Timur's allies, a man who happened to hold a personal blood feud against the fallen amir. Timur was now the undisputed master of Mawarannahr.

In April of 1370, at a grand *qurultai*, or assembly of nobles, held on the plains outside Balkh, Timur had himself proclaimed the supreme ruler. He understood, however, the immense and enduring prestige of the line of Genghis Khan. Not being a direct descendant of the Great Khan, he could not legitimately claim the title of 'Khan' for himself. Instead, he adopted the more modest but militarily potent title of 'Amir'. For the rest of his reign, he maintained a legal fiction, ruling in the name of a puppet Chagatai khan whom he kept as a figurehead at his court. To further cement his connection to the sacred Chinggisid lineage, he married Saray Mulk Khanum, a princess of direct descent. This marriage entitled him to the prestigious title of *Güregen*, or "royal son-in-law," a name he proudly stamped on his coinage.

Having secured his political legitimacy, he turned to creating a capital worthy of his new status. He rejected Bukhara, the city of scholars, and chose instead the ancient and ruined city of

Samarkand. It was here, in the heart of Sogdiana, that he would build a new center for his world empire, a city that would become a byword for opulence and architectural splendor. Samarkand was to be the fixed point in his nomadic universe, the destination for the vast river of wealth that would soon flow from the four corners of the known world.

For the next thirty-five years, Timur waged war on an almost unimaginable scale. His life became a blur of relentless campaigning, his military energy seemingly inexhaustible. His campaigns were not random acts of violence but were part of a grand, if brutal, strategic vision aimed at eliminating all rivals, securing all major trade routes, and making his empire the undisputed center of the world. He first secured his own backyard, launching multiple punishing campaigns into Moghulistan to the east and Khwarazm to the north, ensuring that no threat could emerge from his immediate frontiers.

His most epic struggle was with the Golden Horde and its ambitious ruler, Tokhtamysh. A protégé of Timur's who had been helped to the throne, Tokhtamysh proved an ungrateful and dangerous rival. In 1385, he betrayed his former patron by invading the Caucasus and northern Iran. Timur's response was methodical and utterly devastating. He pursued Tokhtamysh not once, but twice, on epic campaigns that took his army thousands of miles into the unknown northern steppes. In 1391, at the Battle of the Kondurcha River in the heart of modern-day Russia, he crushed the Horde's army. When Tokhtamysh recovered and dared to challenge him again, Timur returned in 1395, met him at the Terek River, and annihilated his forces completely. He then followed up this victory by systematically sacking the great trading cities of the Golden Horde, including its capital, Sarai. The Golden Horde never fully recovered, its power shattered, and the northern branch of the Silk Road was permanently rerouted south, through Timur's domain.

With his northern flank secure, he turned his attention south and west. In a series of massive campaigns, often referred to as the "Three-Year" and "Five-Year" campaigns, he systematically subjugated the entirety of Persia, the Caucasus, and Mesopotamia. The mosaic of petty kingdoms that had emerged from the collapse of the Mongol Ilkhanate was swept away. Timur's method was chillingly effective. Cities that submitted without resistance were spared, though they had to pay a ruinous tribute. Cities that dared to resist were subjected to exemplary terror. After a rebellion in Isfahan in 1387, he ordered a general massacre, and his soldiers were commanded to build pyramids and towers from the severed heads of the city's inhabitants—according to contemporary sources, some 70,000 of them. This was calculated psychological warfare, a message in blood and bone intended to paralyze all future opposition.

In 1398, at the age of sixty-two, when most men would be content with their achievements, Timur embarked on one of his most audacious campaigns: the invasion of India. His stated motivation was to punish the Muslim sultans of Delhi for being too tolerant of their Hindu subjects, casting himself as a *ghazi*, or holy warrior. The true motivation was almost certainly the lure of the legendary wealth of the subcontinent. His army crossed the Hindu Kush and descended onto the plains of India. The army of the Delhi Sultanate, with its fearsome corps of armored war elephants, was crushed outside the city walls. Delhi was then subjected to a sack of such ferocity that, according to one chronicler, "for two whole months, not a bird moved wing in the city." His army returned to Samarkand laden with an incalculable fortune in gold, jewels, and slaves.

His final great series of campaigns took him to the shores of the Mediterranean. He first turned on the Mamluk Sultanate of Egypt and Syria, sacking the ancient cities of Aleppo and Damascus. It was in Damascus that he famously held a series of debates with the great Arab historian and philosopher, Ibn Khaldun, an intellectual sparring match between the world's greatest conqueror and its most profound thinker. From Syria, he moved into Anatolia to confront the rising power of the Ottoman Empire under its formidable sultan, Bayezid I, nicknamed *Yıldırım*, or "the Thunderbolt." The two great Turkic warlords met at the Battle of Ankara in July 1402. In a tactical masterpiece, Timur's army outflanked and overwhelmed the Ottomans. Bayezid himself was captured, the first and only time an Ottoman sultan would be taken prisoner in battle. The Ottoman state was shattered, plunged into a civil war that would set back its expansion for decades and, perhaps inadvertently, grant a reprieve to the beleaguered Byzantine Empire.

Timur was a paradox, a figure of staggering contradictions. The man who ordered the construction of skull towers was also a devoted patron of the arts, architecture, and Islamic learning. His destructive campaigns abroad were matched by a feverish program of construction at home. His grand vision was to make Samarkand the "Pearl of the Eastern World," and he pursued this goal with the same obsessive energy he applied to warfare. His primary method was brutally simple: after conquering a city, he would systematically round up its most skilled architects, artisans, stone masons, tile-makers, calligraphers, and scholars and deport them to his capital.

Samarkand was transformed. A new city wall was built, along with broad avenues and vast public squares. The centerpiece was the Registan, which he began to develop as the city's ceremonial heart. He commissioned the construction of the colossal Bibi-Khanym Mosque, intended to be the largest mosque in the Islamic world, its scale so ambitious that it began to suffer from structural problems almost as soon as it was completed. For himself and his descendants, he ordered the construction of a magnificent mausoleum, the Gur-e-Amir, its fluted turquoise dome destined to become one of the most iconic symbols of Islamic architecture. He laid out enormous pleasure gardens on the outskirts of the city, complete with pavilions and palaces, where he would hold lavish feasts. This explosion of artistic and architectural activity, funded by the plunder of empire and executed by the genius of its captive craftsmen, was the dawn of a Central Asian renaissance.

This cultural flourishing was uniquely Timurid. It was a synthesis of Persian aesthetic traditions with the Turkic taste for monumental scale and grandiose geometry, all executed with a technical virtuosity that was unparalleled. Timur himself was not a scholar, but he was a man of keen intelligence and curiosity. He loved to be read histories of his great predecessors, and he enjoyed conversing with theologians and scientists. He consciously projected an image of himself as both a world-conqueror in the mold of Genghis Khan and a devout Muslim ruler, a champion of the faith. He embodied the Turco-Mongol tradition that had been brewing for a century: he ruled through a Turkic military elite, administered his settled lands with a Persian bureaucracy, and legitimized his power through both the Islamic faith and his connection to the Mongol imperial legacy.

By the winter of 1404, Timur stood at the apex of his power. He had conquered or humbled every major power in the Islamic world. There was, however, one final ambition left to fulfill. For years, he had planned the ultimate campaign: the invasion of Ming China. It was a goal of almost insane ambition, to conquer the most populous and well-organized state on earth. He assembled a gigantic army, perhaps two hundred thousand strong, and in the depths of one of the coldest winters on record, he marched his forces northeast. He reached the old frontier city of Otrar on the Syr Darya, the very place where the diplomatic incident that had triggered the Mongol invasion of his homeland had occurred nearly two centuries earlier. But he would go no further. The harsh winter, combined with his advanced age, proved too much. In February 1405, the Lord of the Fortunate Conjunction, the Flail of God, the master of a ravaged and rebuilt world, died of a fever. The invasion of China was abandoned, and the colossal empire he had forged through a lifetime of violence and vision was immediately thrown into question.

CHAPTER TWELVE: The Legacy of Ulugh Beg and the Timurid Decline

The death of a world-conqueror is always a precarious moment. An empire forged by the singular will and terror of one man rarely survives him intact, and the colossal domain of Amir Timur was no exception. When he died of a fever in the winter of 1405 in the frontier town of Otrar, before he could unleash his final, apocalyptic campaign against Ming China, the news was suppressed for as long as possible. His generals understood that the instant the great Amir's death became known, the bonds of fear and loyalty that held his vast and brutally acquired territories together would snap. And snap they did. The invasion of China was immediately abandoned, and the gargantuan army, now a headless beast, turned back towards Samarkand. The question of succession, which Timur had attempted to settle, was instantly thrown wide open.

Timur had designated his grandson, Pir Muhammad, as his heir. But a deathbed proclamation made hundreds of miles from the capital meant little to the other ambitious princes of the blood, each of whom commanded a powerful army and harbored an outsized sense of his own destiny. The most immediate challenge came from another grandson, Khalil Sultan, who had been with the army at Otrar. In a bold move, he seized the royal treasury, marched on Samarkand, and had himself declared sultan. His reign was a brief and spectacular disaster. He squandered Timur's immense, blood-won fortune on lavish gifts to his supporters and on his favorite wife, a woman of common birth whose influence over him scandalized the Turco-Mongol military elite. The empire, for a moment, seemed destined to dissolve in a blaze of profligacy and incompetence.

The man who would restore a measure of order was Timur's fourth and only surviving son, Shah Rukh. While his father had been a restless conqueror, Shah Rukh was a pious, thoughtful, and statesmanlike figure. At the time of Timur's death, he was the long-serving governor of Khurasan, a vast and wealthy province that he had ruled with a steady and competent hand from its capital, Herat. He watched the chaos in Samarkand with disapproval, patiently consolidating his own power base. By 1409, Khalil Sultan's brief and calamitous reign had collapsed under its own weight. Shah Rukh marched into Mawarannahr, took control of Samarkand, and became the undisputed, if not officially titled, emperor of the Timurid realm.

Shah Rukh's reign marked a profound shift in the character and direction of the empire. He was not his father. He had no taste for endless conquest and pyramids of skulls. His primary interests were in stability, justice, trade, and the patronage of Islamic culture. He abandoned Samarkand as the imperial capital, preferring to rule from his beloved Herat, which he and his remarkable wife, Gawhar Shad, transformed into the new political and cultural heart of the empire. Herat became a city of stunning mosques, madrasas, and libraries, a hub of artistic production, particularly in the fields of miniature painting and calligraphy. Shah Rukh projected an image of himself not as a world-conqueror, but as an ideal Islamic sovereign, a devout and just ruler who promoted peace and prosperity.

He did not, however, abandon Samarkand. He understood its immense strategic and symbolic importance as the city of his father. To govern this crucial northern province of Mawarannahr, he appointed his eldest son, a young man of fifteen named Muhammad Taraghay, better known to history by his nickname, Ulugh Beg, or the "Great Prince." In 1409, Ulugh Beg was installed as the governor of Samarkand, a position he would hold for the next forty years. It was a decision that would create two distinct but linked centers of Timurid power: the political and artistic capital of Herat under the senior emperor Shah Rukh, and the scientific and intellectual capital of Samarkand under his semi-autonomous son, Ulugh Beg.

Like his father, Ulugh Beg was a complete departure from the mold of his grandfather. The ferocious, warlike spirit of Timur seemed to have skipped a generation. Ulugh Beg showed little interest in military campaigning or the brutal politics of the Turco-Mongol amirs. His passions lay not in the mastery of the battlefield but in the mastery of the heavens. From a young age, he was captivated by mathematics and astronomy, a fascination perhaps sparked by a visit as a boy to the ruins of a great observatory in Maragheh, built by the Mongol Ilkhans in Persia. While his father focused on running the empire, Ulugh Beg dedicated the immense resources of his province to the pursuit of knowledge. He was to become the scholar-king par excellence.

His first major act of patronage was not for a palace, but for a place of learning. In 1417, he began the construction of a magnificent madrasa on the western side of the Registan square, the great public plaza of Samarkand. This was to be no ordinary religious seminary. Ulugh Beg intended it to be a true university, an institute for the advanced study of both the theological and the rational sciences. The grand portal of the madrasa was decorated with a mosaic of stars against a deep blue background, a clear statement of its founder's astronomical interests. An inscription above the entrance declared that "The search for knowledge is an obligation of every Muslim man and woman," a powerful endorsement of intellectual inquiry. He gathered the finest scholarly minds from across the Islamic world to teach there, and he himself is said to have occasionally delivered lectures.

The madrasa was merely a prelude to his life's great work. Ulugh Beg's ultimate ambition was to correct and update the astronomical tables of the past, to create a definitive map of the heavens that would be more accurate than any that had come before. To do this, he required instruments of a scale and precision never previously attempted. Around 1424, on a hill overlooking Samarkand, he began the construction of a monumental observatory, the *Gurkhani Zij*. It was a scientific instrument on an architectural scale. The centerpiece of the three-story cylindrical building was a colossal Fakhri sextant, a gigantic stone arc with a radius of over forty meters, set deep into a trench dug into the hillside. This immense instrument, aligned perfectly with the north-south meridian, allowed for extraordinarily precise measurements of the transit of the sun, moon, and planets as they crossed the celestial meridian, enabling calculations of their altitude with unprecedented accuracy.

Ulugh Beg did not work in isolation. He was the patron and director of a collaborative scientific enterprise, a veritable academy of sciences. He assembled a team of the most brilliant mathematicians and astronomers of his day. Among them were Ghiyath al-Din Jamshid al-Kashi, a mathematical genius who made significant advances in the calculation of pi and the solution of cubic equations; Qadi Zada al-Rumi, a distinguished scholar from Anatolia; and, after their deaths, the brilliant Ali Qushji, who would become Ulugh Beg's most trusted collaborator. For nearly two decades, this team worked relentlessly, making nightly observations, performing complex trigonometric calculations, and compiling their results.

The fruit of this monumental labor was the *Zij-i Sultani*, or "The Sultan's Astronomical Tables," completed around 1437. It was the crowning scientific achievement of the Timurid era and one of the most important works of observational astronomy of the entire pre-telescopic age. The *Zij* contained the most comprehensive and accurate star catalog produced between the time of the ancient Greek astronomer Ptolemy and the Danish astronomer Tycho Brahe over a century later. It meticulously listed the positions of 1,018 stars, with a level of precision that was astonishing for its time. It also included highly accurate calculations for the length of the sidereal year, determining it to be 365 days, 6 hours, 10 minutes, and 8 seconds—a value only about a minute longer than the modern calculation. It also established the Earth's axial tilt with remarkable precision.

Ulugh Beg's court was a haven for science, but his obsession with the stars came at a cost. His deep immersion in intellectual pursuits left him ill-suited for the harsh realities of governing a Central Asian province. He was, by all accounts, a poor general and an indecisive political leader. He lacked the ruthlessness and martial vigor that the Turco-Mongol military aristocracy, the amirs, expected from a Timurid prince. His immense expenditures on his madrasa and observatory, while culturally priceless, were seen by some as a wasteful diversion of state funds. More dangerously, his scientific work and his deep interest in astrology—he was said to have cast a horoscope predicting his own son would cause his death—aroused the suspicion of the conservative Islamic clergy. They viewed his focus on the rational sciences as bordering on heresy, a distraction from true faith.

While the astronomers of Samarkand charted the heavens, a new and dangerous storm was gathering on the northern horizon. The nomadic Uzbek tribes of the steppe, who had been shattered by Timur, were coalescing once more under a new and powerful leader, Abul-Khayr Khan. Throughout the 1430s and 1440s, these Uzbeks began to launch increasingly bold and damaging raids into the cultivated lands of Mawarannahr, threatening the very foundations of the Timurid state. Ulugh Beg's military responses to these incursions were consistently inept and unsuccessful, further eroding his authority in the eyes of the military elite. He was a master of the celestial sphere, but on the terrestrial plane, his grip was slipping.

The fragile stability of the empire depended entirely on the authority of one man: the aged emperor Shah Rukh in Herat. When he finally died in 1447 at the age of seventy, the last check on the ambitions of the younger Timurid princes was removed. The empire was immediately plunged into the very kind of succession crisis he had worked so hard to prevent. Ulugh Beg, as the senior surviving prince, had the strongest claim to the throne, but his authority was not respected. He found himself embroiled in a debilitating war with his own relatives, particularly a nephew in Herat, for control of the wider empire.

The most fatal threat, however, came not from a nephew, but from his own son, Abd al-Latif. The relationship between father and son had soured badly. Abd al-Latif was an accomplished soldier who felt his father neither trusted nor respected him. He was a devout Muslim, more aligned with the conservative clergy than with his father's scientific circle. Sensing an opportunity, the disaffected military amirs and religious leaders rallied around the resentful son, encouraging him to rebel. In 1449, the unthinkable happened:

the son declared war on the father. The two armies met in battle near Samarkand. Ulugh Beg's forces, poorly led and unmotivated, were defeated. The scholar-king was forced to surrender to his own child.

The final act of the tragedy was swift and brutal. Abd al-Latif, now the master of Samarkand, gave his sanction for his father's execution. On the pretense of allowing him to make the pilgrimage to Mecca, Ulugh Beg was led to a small village outside the capital. There, in the autumn of 1449, the man who had measured the stars was forced to his knees and beheaded. The murder of a father by a son was a shocking act that horrified even the war-hardened society of the time. Abd al-Latif's bloody reign lasted only six months before he was assassinated in a palace coup organized by the very amirs who had helped him to power.

The death of Ulugh Beg marked the beginning of the end for the Timurid empire in Mawarannahr. Samarkand was plunged into a period of chaotic, violent turmoil as petty princes and powerful amirs fought over the scraps of a dying state. The great observatory, the symbol of Ulugh Beg's reign, was sacked and fell into ruin, its scientific work abandoned. It was so completely destroyed that its exact location would be lost for over four hundred years, until its foundations were rediscovered by an archaeologist in 1908. One of its greatest minds, Ali Qushji, managed to escape the chaos, taking with him a precious copy of the *Zij-i Sultani*. He eventually found refuge at the court of the Ottoman Sultan Mehmed the Conqueror in Istanbul, ensuring that Ulugh Beg's astronomical legacy would survive and eventually filter into Europe. But in its homeland, the brief, brilliant light of the Samarkand school was extinguished. The Timurid state in Mawarannahr, fatally weakened by internal rot and fratricidal conflict, was now a hollow shell, waiting for a final push from the Uzbeks gathering on the steppe.

CHAPTER THIRTEEN: The Shaybanids and the Establishment of Uzbek Khanates

The final half-century of Timurid rule in Mawarannahr was a slow, agonizing bleed. The fratricidal chaos that followed the murder of the astronomer-king Ulugh Beg in 1449 had shattered any semblance of centralized authority. In the once-mighty capital of Samarkand and the fading cultural center of Herat, Timurid princelings, each claiming a sliver of the conqueror's prestige, engaged in a dizzying and destructive ballet of intrigue and warfare. They were peacocks fighting over the ruins of a palace, oblivious to the wolves gathering on the horizon. While they exhausted their resources in petty squabbles, the political and demographic landscape of the great northern steppe, the Dasht-i-Kipchak, was undergoing a momentous consolidation. A new, hard-bitten power was on the rise, and its people were known as the Uzbeks.

The term "Uzbek" was not new. It had been used for centuries as a general name for the Turkic and Turco-Mongol warrior nomads of the steppes that had once formed the eastern wing of the Golden Horde. They were a loose confederation of tribes, the inheritors of a martial tradition stretching back to the sons of Genghis Khan. For generations, they had lived a life of pastoral nomadism, occasionally raiding their settled neighbors to the south but lacking the unity to pose an existential threat. This changed dramatically in the mid-fifteenth century with the rise of a leader of formidable ambition and skill: Abul-Khayr Khan. A direct descendant of Genghis Khan through his grandson Shayban, Abul-Khayr possessed the pedigree and the prowess to unite the disparate tribes. Beginning in 1428, he embarked on a four-decade-long career of conquest, forging the scattered clans into a powerful nomadic empire that stretched from the Aral Sea to the edge of Siberia.

Abul-Khayr's Uzbek confederation became the dominant power of the steppe. As Ulugh Beg's authority crumbled, he saw his opportunity, launching a series of punishing raids deep into Mawarannahr. He sacked the towns ringing the great oases, carried off slaves and plunder, and demonstrated with each incursion the military impotence of the feuding Timurid princes. For a time, it seemed as if he would be the one to sweep away the remnants of Timur's empire. But the inherent fragility of steppe confederations proved to be his undoing. His attempts to centralize power were resented by rival chieftains, and a catastrophic defeat at the hands of a rival nomadic group, the Oirats, in 1457 shattered his prestige. His long reign ended in 1468 with his death in battle, and his powerful empire immediately disintegrated, its constituent tribes scattering to the four winds. The Uzbek moment seemed to have passed.

Among the many who suffered in the collapse of Abul-Khayr's state were his young son and grandson. His grandson, Muhammad Shaybani, born around 1451, was cast into the unforgiving world of the post-imperial steppe. His youth was a brutal education in survival. His father was killed, and he and his brother became fugitives, landless princes with a distinguished lineage but no army. For nearly two decades, he was a soldier of fortune, a minor player in the great game of Central Asian politics. He sold his sword to the highest bidder, serving as a mercenary captain for various Timurid princes and for the Moghul khans in the east. It was a humiliating but invaluable apprenticeship. He learned the art of war firsthand, studied the internal weaknesses of his enemies, and cultivated a core of fiercely loyal followers. Above all, he nursed a burning ambition: to reclaim his grandfather's legacy, reunite the Uzbek tribes, and seize the rich, decaying lands of Mawarannahr for himself.

By the 1490s, the situation in the south had reached a terminal stage of decay. The last generation of Timurids had produced a final, remarkable figure in Zahir-ud-din Muhammad Babur, the ruler of the small principality of Ferghana. Babur was a man of immense culture, a gifted poet and diarist, but also a brave and resourceful commander. He was, however, just one of a dozen contenders in a free-for-all. While Babur and his relatives fought over the control of Samarkand, passing the city back and forth between them, Muhammad Shaybani was patiently reassembling the pieces of his grandfather's confederation. He rallied the scattered Uzbek tribes under his banner, winning their allegiance through force of personality and the promise of rich plunder to the south. By the turn of the century, he had forged a new, formidable Uzbek army, hardened by steppe warfare and eager for conquest.

In 1500, Shaybani Khan made his move. He swept down from the north, his target the heart of the Timurid realm. The Timurid princes, unable to put aside their rivalries to face the common threat, were picked off one by one. Shaybani's first major prize was Bukhara. He then marched on the great capital of Samarkand, which was then held by one of Babur's cousins. The city, weary of the endless civil war, surrendered with little resistance. Muhammad Shaybani, the landless fugitive, rode in triumph into the city of Amir Timur.

The young Babur, however, was not finished. In a daring winter raid later that year, he and a small band of followers scaled the walls of Samarkand and retook the city, its people welcoming him as a liberator from the rough-mannered Uzbeks. It was a fleeting, romantic victory. Babur held the city for a few months, but he was isolated and without allies. In the spring of 1501, Shaybani returned with his main army and besieged the city. After a disastrous defeat in open battle, Babur was trapped. The siege dragged on for six months, and with starvation setting in, Babur was forced to concede defeat. He negotiated a humiliating treaty, giving his sister in marriage to his rival in exchange for safe passage. He slipped out of the city at night, a fugitive once again, his dream of ruling his ancestral homeland shattered. He would eventually turn his ambitions south, towards India, where he would go on to found the great Mughal Empire. His departure marked the end of Timurid rule in Central Asia.

With Mawarannahr secured, Shaybani was relentless. In 1505, he turned his attention to Khwarazm, conquering its capital, Gurganj, and adding the ancient oasis to his growing domain. His final prize was Khurasan, the last major Timurid principality, ruled from Herat by Sultan Husayn Bayqara, a celebrated patron of the arts.

When the aged Sultan died in 1506, his sons fell to quarreling over the succession, providing Shaybani with the perfect pretext to invade. In 1507, the Uzbeks marched into Herat, the cultural jewel of the late Timurid world, without a fight. In less than a decade, Muhammad Shaybani had extinguished the century-old empire of Timur and established a new Uzbek empire in its place.

The new state was a dramatic departure from the centralized, Persianate bureaucracy of the late Timurids. Shaybani and his followers were nomads, and they brought the political traditions of the steppe with them. The empire was not viewed as the personal property of the khan but as the collective inheritance of the entire ruling clan. This led to the immediate implementation of an appanage system. Conquered territories were not integrated into a central administration but were parceled out as semi-independent fiefdoms to Shaybani's brothers, uncles, nephews, and other leading sultans. Shaybani, as the supreme Khan, retained overall authority and ruled from the symbolic capital of Samarkand, but his relatives governed their own territories, minted their own coins, and maintained their own armies. This system, while ensuring the loyalty of the ruling elite, also sowed the seeds of future fragmentation and internal conflict.

A new ruling class was imposed on the region. The Uzbek military aristocracy, speaking Chagatai Turkic, replaced the old Turco-Mongol elite of the Timurids. They took over the most productive agricultural lands as their personal estates and established themselves as the unquestioned masters of the sedentary, Persian-speaking population of the cities and villages. There was a palpable cultural shift. The refined, high-minded artistic culture of the late Timurid courts in Herat gave way to the more austere, martial, and orthodox Islamic values of the Uzbeks.

Shaybani's triumphs had made him the most powerful Sunni ruler of his day, but his conquests had also brought him into direct contact with a new and formidable power rising in the west. In Persia, a charismatic and messianic leader named Ismail had founded the Safavid Empire. Ismail was not just a conqueror; he was the head of a militant Sufi order who declared himself the hidden Imam and imposed Twelver Shi'ism as the official state religion of Iran. This created a profound and violent sectarian rift in the heart of the Islamic world. For the staunchly Sunni Uzbeks, the Shi'a Safavids were not just political rivals; they were dangerous heretics. A collision was inevitable.

The flashpoint was Khurasan. For Shah Ismail, the province was a historic part of the Iranian world that had to be reclaimed. For Shaybani Khan, it was a recent and valuable conquest and a bastion of Sunnism. After a series of border skirmishes and increasingly insulting diplomatic exchanges, Shah Ismail decided to act. In 1510, he marched east with a large, disciplined army equipped with firearms, a technology the Uzbeks largely lacked. He laid siege to the city of Merv, where Shaybani had taken up position.

Shaybani, a master of mobile steppe warfare, was wary of the Safavid army's firepower and refused to be drawn into a pitched battle. Shah Ismail then employed a clever ruse. Feigning a retreat, he lured the overconfident Uzbeks out from behind their defenses. Shaybani, believing the Safavids were in flight, gave chase with a smaller contingent of his army, only to be ambushed by the main Safavid force. The Uzbek cavalry was surrounded and annihilated. Shaybani Khan was killed in the fighting. His demise was followed by an act of symbolic brutality that echoed through the centuries. Shah Ismail had the Uzbek khan's body dismembered; his hands were sent to rival rulers as a warning, and his skull, inlaid with gold, was fashioned into a drinking goblet for the victorious Shah.

The death of its founder and the destruction of its army was a catastrophic blow to the new Uzbek state. The empire collapsed almost as quickly as it had been built. Shah Ismail's Safavid forces swept into Khurasan and even crossed the Amu Darya, occupying Bukhara and Samarkand. For a brief, heady moment, it seemed as if the Safavids would become the new masters of Mawarannahr. They even had an ally: Babur, who, seeing his old nemesis dead, returned from Kabul at the head of an army, hoping to reclaim his ancestral throne as a Safavid vassal.

The Uzbek cause, however, was not extinguished. The appanage system, which had been a source of weakness, now proved to be a source of resilience. While the main khan was dead, the other Shaybanid sultans still commanded their own forces in their respective territories. The leadership of the resistance fell to Shaybani's capable nephew, Ubaydullah, who had been governing Bukhara. Ubaydullah Khan was a shrewd politician and a determined warrior, a man who combined his uncle's military energy with a deep personal piety. He rallied the scattered Uzbek forces, capitalizing on the deep resentment of the local Sunni population towards the occupying Shi'a Safavids and their Timurid puppet, Babur.

The Safavid-Babur occupation was short-lived. The imposition of Shi'a practices in deeply Sunni cities like Samarkand provoked widespread popular discontent. Ubaydullah harnessed this religious anger and, in a series of brilliant campaigns, pushed the invaders back. In 1512, at the Battle of Ghujduvan near Bukhara, the Uzbeks won a decisive victory over a combined Safavid-Baburid army. The Safavid commander was killed, and Babur was forced to flee Mawarannahr for the last time. The brief Safavid interlude was over, and Uzbek rule was firmly re-established.

In the decades that followed, Ubaydullah Khan worked to consolidate the state his uncle had founded. He spent much of his reign in a constant, grinding war with the Safavids over control of Khurasan, a conflict that would define the region's political geography for the next two centuries. While he never succeeded in permanently retaking Herat, he successfully defended Mawarannahr from any further Safavid incursions, cementing the Amu Darya as the fortified frontier between the Sunni Turkic world of Central Asia and the Shi'a Persian world of Iran.

Recognizing the strategic and commercial importance of his own former appanage, Ubaydullah gradually shifted the political center of gravity away from Samarkand. He ruled from Bukhara, adorning it with mosques and madrasas and making it the de facto capital of the Uzbek state. This move was finalized by his successors. Under Abdullah Khan II, a long and powerful reign in the latter half of the sixteenth century, the state was officially known as the Khanate of Bukhara. The initial, sprawling empire of Muhammad Shaybani had begun its long transformation into a more compact, stable, and enduring political entity, a state that would shape the religious and cultural life of the region for generations. Other Shaybanid lines would establish a rival khanate in Khwarazm, but it was Bukhara that would become the heart of the new Uzbek order.

CHAPTER FOURTEEN: The Khanate of Bukhara: A Center of Islamic Learning

The death of the fearsome Muhammad Shaybani Khan in a golden drinking goblet and the subsequent rout of his armies might have signaled the end of the fledgling Uzbek state. But the house that Shaybani built, while shaken to its foundations, did not fall. The brief, humiliating occupation of Samarkand by the Shi'a Safavids and their Timurid puppet, Babur, had the opposite of its intended effect. It galvanized the Sunni population, outraged their religious sensibilities, and united the disparate Uzbek princes behind a common cause. When Shaybani's nephew, Ubaydullah Khan, drove the invaders out in 1512, he was not just reclaiming territory; he was positioning his dynasty as the indispensable champion of Sunni orthodoxy in a world newly fractured by sectarian strife. This role, as the staunch defender of the faith against the heretics of Persia, would come to define the new political entity he helped forge: the Khanate of Bukhara.

Although Samarkand remained the symbolic Timurid capital for a time, the political and spiritual center of gravity steadily shifted west. Ubaydullah, a pious and learned man in his own right, preferred to rule from his former appanage of Bukhara. It was a shrewd choice. Bukhara had a venerable history as a center of Islamic scholarship, a reputation that predated even the Samanids. Under Ubaydullah and his successors, this reputation was deliberately cultivated. The city was to be more than just a capital; it was to be a bastion, the *Qubbat al-Islam*, or "Dome of Islam," in the East. This was not mere propaganda. It was a conscious political strategy aimed at legitimizing Uzbek rule, not through the fading memory of Chinggisid or Timurid conquest, but through the potent currency of religious authority.

The state was ruled for nearly a century by the descendants of Shayban, but the nomadic appanage system was a constant source of instability. The realm was seen as the shared property of the royal clan, with various sultans governing their territories with a high degree of autonomy. This created a permanent state of latent civil war, as ambitious cousins and nephews frequently battled for the supreme title of Khan. It was only under the long and iron-fisted reign of Abdullah Khan II, from 1583 to 1598, that the Khanate was truly unified. A ruthless and energetic ruler, Abdullah Khan crushed his relatives, centralized the administration, and waged successful wars against the Safavids. He definitively established Bukhara as the one and only capital, embarking on a massive building program that transformed its urban landscape. His reign represented the zenith of Shaybanid power, a brief golden age of stability and prosperity.

This unity did not long survive him. When the last Shaybanid ruler died without a male heir in 1601, the dynasty came to an end. Power passed, not through conquest, but through genealogy. The new khans came from the Janid or Astrakhanid dynasty, so named because they were descendants of the khans of Astrakhan on the Volga River, who themselves traced their lineage back to Jochi, the eldest son of Genghis Khan. Their claim to the throne of Bukhara was through the female line, via a marriage to the family of Abdullah Khan II. This transition ensured the continuity of the Chinggisid tradition, but it did little to solve the state's underlying structural weaknesses. The Janid khans, like their predecessors, would spend much of their time trying to assert their authority over powerful and recalcitrant Uzbek tribal leaders.

Throughout these dynastic shifts and political struggles, the project of turning Bukhara into a great center of learning continued unabated. The Uzbek khans, whatever their political shortcomings, were lavish patrons of religious architecture. They understood that constructing a grand madrasa or a magnificent mosque was a statement of power and piety that resonated deeply with their subjects. Ubaydullah Khan himself commissioned the splendid Mir-i-Arab Madrasa, which still stands opposite the Kalyan Mosque, its twin blue domes a defining feature of the city's skyline. Under Abdullah Khan II, the city's commercial heart was given its iconic form with the construction of domed bazaars and caravanserais. The Janids continued this tradition, with the Abdulaziz Khan Madrasa, built in the seventeenth century, representing the last great masterpiece of the Bukharan architectural style, its portal a riot of colorful and intricate tilework.

These buildings were the physical manifestation of the city's purpose. The madrasas were the engines of its intellectual and spiritual life. From all over the Muslim world, but especially from the Turkic-speaking lands to the north and east, students flocked to Bukhara. Tatars from the Volga, Kazakhs from the steppes, and Muslims from as far away as Kashgar and Siberia came to study at the feet of its famous scholars. The curriculum was deeply conservative, focused on the preservation and transmission of established Islamic knowledge. The core subjects were the Qur'an and its interpretation (*tafsir*), the traditions of the Prophet (*hadith*), and, above all, Islamic jurisprudence (*fiqh*), according to the Hanafi school of law, which was dominant in Central Asia. This was not an environment that fostered the kind of scientific innovation seen under Ulugh Beg; its purpose was to produce qualified judges, teachers, and imams who would uphold the standards of Sunni orthodoxy throughout the region.

Looming even larger than the formal scholarship of the madrasas was the pervasive influence of Sufism. The mystical brotherhoods, or *tariqas*, held immense power in the Khanate. By far the most powerful of these was the Naqshbandi order, which had originated in the countryside around Bukhara in the fourteenth century. The tomb of the order's founder, Baha-ud-Din Naqshband, located just outside the city, was the most sacred shrine in the region, a major center of pilgrimage. The Naqshbandi sheikhs were more than just spiritual guides; they were immense political and economic players. They owned vast tracts of tax-exempt land (*waqf*), controlled extensive commercial networks, and served as the trusted, and sometimes feared, advisors to the khans.

The support of the leading Naqshbandi sheikhs could make or break a ruler. They were the ultimate legitimizers of power, their blessing a crucial prerequisite for a successful reign. This gave them an authority that often rivaled that of the khan himself. Their brand of Sufism was sober, sharia-compliant, and deeply embedded in the political establishment, a stark contrast to some of the more ecstatic and populist Sufi movements. This deep-rooted connection between the state and the religious establishment created a profoundly conservative society, one in which the authority of the khan, the amirs, and the sheikhs was mutually reinforcing.

Life in the Khanate was sustained by the ancient rhythms of the oasis. The economy rested on the irrigated agriculture of the Zarafshan river valley, where peasants cultivated wheat, cotton, and the melons for which the region was famous. While the great transcontinental Silk Road had been largely supplanted by maritime routes, regional trade remained vibrant. Bukharan caravans plied the routes north to Russia, exchanging cotton textiles and handcrafted goods for furs, leather, and manufactured items. Trade with Mughal India to the south was brisk, with merchants traversing the difficult passes of the Hindu Kush. Despite the bitter sectarian hostility, a surprising amount of commerce continued with Safavid Iran, a testament to the fact that profit often speaks louder than piety. The city of Bukhara itself was a cosmopolitan hub, its bazaars filled not only with local Tajik and Uzbek traders but also with communities of Indians and the famously resourceful Bukharan Jews, who played a key role in the city's financial and commercial life.

The society was a distinct hierarchy. At the top was the ruling Uzbek military elite, organized into tribes and clans, whose leaders, the amirs, held the key military and administrative posts. They were the landowning aristocracy, and their primary language was Chagatai Turkic. The bulk of the urban population, including the merchants, artisans, and the all-important bureaucracy, were largely Persian-speaking Tajiks, often referred to as Sarts. They were the inheritors of the ancient sedentary culture of the region, the people who kept the cities running. The countryside was populated by a mixture of Tajik and Uzbek farmers, their lives dictated by the flow of water in the irrigation canals and the demands of the tax collector.

For all its religious prestige and commercial vitality, the Khanate was politically brittle. The Janid dynasty, lacking the fearsome authority of the early Shaybanids, was never able to fully master the powerful Uzbek tribal chieftains. The seventeenth and early eighteenth centuries were marked by a steady erosion of central authority. Powerful amirs, ruling their domains as virtual kings, frequently defied the khan in Bukhara and waged war on one another. The title of *ataliq*, originally meaning a royal tutor, was usurped by the leaders of the most powerful tribes, who became the de facto rulers, treating the Janid khans as mere puppets. The state was slowly dissolving from within, its military strength sapped by endless internal conflict.

The final, decisive blow came from outside. In Persia, a brilliant and ruthless military adventurer named Nadir Shah had restored the country's fortunes and embarked on a career of conquest that rivaled that of Timur. He saw the weak and divided Khanate of Bukhara as an easy target. In 1740, Nadir Shah crossed the Amu Darya with a large, modern army equipped with artillery. The Bukharan forces, plagued by internal disunity, were in no state to resist. The Janid khan, Abulfayz, offered a humiliating submission. Bukhara was spared a sack, but it was effectively reduced to a vassal state of Persia. The khan became a puppet, and Nadir Shah's authority was absolute.

Nadir Shah's assassination in 1747 created a power vacuum that the Janids were too weak to fill. Real power in Bukhara had already fallen into the hands of the *ataliq* from the powerful Manghit tribe, Muhammad Rahim Biy. For several years, he ruled from behind the throne, content with the title of chief minister. He was the kingmaker, deposing the last Janid puppets at will. Finally, in 1756, he dispensed with the fiction, executing the last Janid ruler and assuming power in his own right, though he initially refused the title of khan. The final step was taken by his successor in 1785, who formally abolished the old Khanate and proclaimed a new state: the Emirate of Bukhara. The long era that had begun with the Shaybanid conquest was over. Bukhara would remain a center of Islamic learning, but its political form had changed, setting the stage for the final act of its pre-colonial history.

CHAPTER FIFTEEN: The Khanates of Khiva and Kokand: Rival Powers in the Region

While the Manghit emirs and Naqshbandi sheikhs of Bukhara were cementing their city's reputation as the Dome of Islam, they were by no means the undisputed masters of the wider region. The dream of a unified Uzbek state, which had briefly flickered into life under Muhammad Shaybani Khan and been revived by Abdullah Khan II, had long since died. The political reality of Central Asia from the sixteenth century until the Russian conquest was one of fragmentation and fierce competition. Bukhara may have been the oldest and most prestigious of the Uzbek states, but it was not the only one. Two other formidable powers, born of the same Turco-Mongol heritage but forged in different environments, carved out their own domains and pursued their own destinies. To the west, in the ancient and isolated oasis of Khwarazm, rose the Khanate of Khiva, a state built on irrigation, tribal politics, and a brutal trade in human lives. To the east, in the fertile and dynamic Ferghana Valley, the Khanate of Kokand would emerge much later, a brash and expansionist upstart that would challenge Bukhara for supremacy. The history of the region in this era is the story of this tripartite rivalry, a relentless three-way struggle for power, territory, and resources.

The origins of an independent state in Khwarazm were a direct consequence of the Shaybanid appanage system. When Muhammad Shaybani conquered the region, he, like his Timurid predecessors, understood that Khwarazm was a world apart, too distant and distinct to be easily ruled from Samarkand or Bukhara. It was therefore granted as a fiefdom to a separate branch of the Shaybanid clan. This arrangement quickly evolved into de facto independence. The Amu Darya river, the lifeblood of the oasis, also served as a formidable political and military barrier, and the rulers of Khwarazm soon began to chart their own course.

Their initial history was turbulent, marked by the same internal Shaybanid squabbles that plagued Mawarannahr. A more stable dynasty, the Arabshahids, another line claiming descent from Genghis Khan through Shayban, took control in the mid-sixteenth century. It was under their rule that a critical event reshaped the geography and politics of the oasis. The unpredictable Amu Darya, in one of its periodic shifts, altered its course, leaving the old and magnificent capital of Gurganj (or Urgench) stranded and with a precarious water supply. In 1598, the capital was permanently moved to a smaller, but better-sited and more defensible town a short distance to the south: Khiva. From this point on, the state would be known by the name of its new capital.

The Khanate of Khiva was a state defined by its geography. Its existence depended entirely on the waters of the Amu Darya, which fanned out into a delta of canals and irrigated fields, creating a patch of vibrant green surrounded by the immense and hostile Karakum and Kyzylkum deserts. This isolation bred a fierce independence but also a profound vulnerability. The khanate's agricultural heartland was a tempting target for the nomadic Turkmen tribes who roamed the desert frontiers, and Khivan history is a near-constant story of conflict and accommodation with these powerful and unruly neighbors.

Over time, real power in the khanate, as in Bukhara, slipped from the hands of the Chinggisid khans to the leaders of the most powerful Uzbek tribes. In Khiva, the dominant tribe was the Qungrat (or Kungrad). By the mid-eighteenth century, the Qungrat chieftains were ruling as *inaqs*, or chief ministers, treating the Arabshahid khans as mere figureheads. This fiction was finally abandoned in 1804 when the Qungrat leader Iltuzar declared himself Khan, establishing a new, non-Chinggisid dynasty that would rule Khiva until the Russian Revolution.

The Khivan economy had two pillars, one respectable and one utterly notorious. The first was agriculture. An army of laborers, many of them slaves, maintained the intricate network of canals that irrigated the fields of wheat, barley, and cotton. The second, and for much of its history more lucrative, pillar was the slave trade. Khiva was, without exaggeration, the greatest slave market in Central Asia. Its power and prosperity were built on the brutal practice of slave raiding. Khivan raiding parties, often composed of allied Turkmen horsemen who were paid for their services, would launch deep forays into the northeastern Persian province of Khurasan. They would sweep down on unsuspecting villages, killing the men who resisted and carrying off thousands of women and children on a perilous journey across the desert. These unfortunate captives, along with Russian fishermen seized on the Caspian Sea and any other travelers unlucky enough to fall into their hands, were then sold in the open markets of Khiva.

This vile trade defined the khanate's relationship with its neighbors. It ensured a state of perpetual, low-grade warfare with Persia and was the primary source of friction with the expanding Russian Empire, which was increasingly incensed by the enslavement of its subjects. The institution of slavery was deeply embedded in Khivan society. Slaves provided the labor for the great construction projects, tilled the fields, and served in the households of the elite. The state was, in many ways, a predatory one, surviving by parasitizing its neighbors.

The internal politics of the khanate were notoriously fractious. The Khivan state was less a unified entity and more a tense confederation of powerful Uzbek tribes—the Qungrats, an ethnic mix of other Uzbek clans, Turkmen, and Karakalpaks—and the settled, largely Persian-speaking population known as Sarts. The khan's authority was constantly being tested by tribal chieftains, who often commanded more loyalty from their own kinsmen than did the ruler in his capital. Revolts were frequent, and the political history of the khanate is a tangled web of tribal rivalries and violent succession struggles.

Despite this instability, the Qungrat khans were ambitious builders. They turned their capital, Khiva, into a unique and perfectly preserved museum of Central Asian Islamic architecture. The heart of the city was the Ichan Kala, a formidable rectangular fortress enclosed by thick, sloping mud-brick walls. Within these walls, successive khans built a stunning ensemble of mosques, madrasas, palaces, and mausoleums. Unlike the grand, monumental style of Samarkand, Khivan architecture was more intimate and ornate, characterized by its brilliant turquoise and cobalt blue tilework, intricately carved wooden columns, and soaring, slender minarets. The stubby but beautifully tiled Kalta Minor minaret, the lavishly decorated Tosh Hovli Palace, and the Juma Mosque with its forest of over two hundred unique wooden pillars, all testify to the wealth, piety, and artistic vision of the Khivan rulers.

While Khiva was an ancient power rooted in the traditions of the oasis, the Khanate of Kokand was a newcomer, a product of the political vacuum of the eighteenth century. Its domain was the Ferghana Valley, a geographic jewel blessed with fertile soil, an abundance of water from the tributaries of the Syr Darya, and a dense, industrious population. The valley had always been a distinct region, but for centuries it had been a dependency of more powerful states, most recently the Khanate of Bukhara. As Bukharan power waned in the early 1700s, local leaders in the Ferghana began to assert their independence.

The dynasty that would come to dominate the valley, the Mings, were leaders of an Uzbek tribe that had settled in the region. Their rise was slow and methodical. The founder of their power, Shahrukh Biy, established his authority around the town of Kokand in the 1720s. He and his immediate successors were careful to pay nominal allegiance to Bukhara, styling themselves simply as *biy* or *beg*, local lords, not as sovereign khans. They focused on consolidating their control over the valley, subduing rival chieftains, and building a strong economic and military base.

The crucial break with the past came with their outright rejection of the Chinggisid principle. Unlike the rulers of Bukhara and Khiva, who for centuries felt compelled to rule through either genuine or puppet descendants of Genghis Khan, the Mings of Kokand based their legitimacy on their own power and on the sanction of Islam. When the ruler Alim Khan formally adopted the title of Khan around 1805, he was making a bold statement: a new power, unconstrained by the old traditions of the steppe, had arrived.

The Khanate of Kokand was an energetic and aggressive state from the outset. Its rulers possessed a keen understanding of the region's economic geography. The Ferghana Valley was not just an agricultural heartland; it was the gateway to the east. By controlling the mountain passes leading to Kashgaria, Kokand dominated the lucrative caravan trade with China. To the north, the valley opened onto the vast Kazakh steppes, providing access to the growing trade with the Russian empire. The khans of Kokand were not content to simply tax this trade; they sought to conquer and control the routes themselves.

Under a series of ambitious and often ruthless rulers, the khanate embarked on a dramatic course of expansion. Alim Khan, a brutal but effective centralizer, created a disciplined standing army and used it to conquer the great commercial city of Tashkent, a prize long contested with Bukhara. His brother and successor, Umar Khan, was a more refined figure, a poet and a lavish patron of the arts who adorned Kokand with elegant mosques and madrasas, attempting to build a capital that could rival Bukhara in its splendor. It was under Umar's son, Muhammad Ali Khan, known as Madali Khan, that the khanate reached its territorial zenith in the 1830s. He extended Kokandian control far to the north, forcing many Kazakh and Kyrgyz tribes to pay him tribute and establishing a series of forts to protect the caravan routes. For a brief period, Kokand was the most powerful and extensive of the three khanates.

This rapid expansion created a permanent and bitter rivalry with Bukhara. The emirs of Bukhara, particularly the cruel and ambitious Emir Nasrullah, viewed the rise of Kokand with alarm. They saw the Kokandian khans as upstarts and rebels, and they considered cities like Tashkent to be their own by right. The first half of the nineteenth century was dominated by the almost constant warfare between the two states. They fought over Tashkent, Khojand, Jizzakh, and Ura-Tepe, with these strategic cities changing hands multiple times. This endless conflict drained the resources of both khanates and created a zone of instability and destruction between them.

The internal politics of Kokand were even more volatile and bloody than those of its rivals. While the khans were more autocratic, the lack of a legitimizing Chinggisid lineage meant that any powerful general or ambitious relative could make a bid for the throne. The state was plagued by a succession of palace coups, assassinations, and civil wars that were breathtaking in their frequency and brutality. This internal rot reached a crisis point under Madali Khan, whose dissolute lifestyle and political missteps alienated both the clergy and the military.

Seeing his rival weakened, Emir Nasrullah of Bukhara decided to strike a decisive blow. In 1842, he invaded the Khanate of Kokand, capitalizing on the widespread discontent with Madali Khan's rule. The Bukharan army took the capital with little resistance. What followed was an act of shocking brutality, even by the standards of the time. Nasrullah had Madali Khan, his brother, and his mother, the celebrated poet-queen Nodira, publicly executed in the main square of Kokand. He then installed a puppet governor and incorporated Kokand into his own domains.

The Bukharan occupation, however, lasted only a few months. The people of Ferghana, who had chafed under their own rulers, found the rule of the Bukharans even more intolerable. A popular uprising, led by a cousin of the murdered khan, drove the Bukharan garrisons out and restored the independence of the khanate. But the state never recovered from this catastrophe. The invasion had exposed its fundamental weakness, and the restored khanate was a hotbed of factionalism and intrigue. The next two decades were a period of near-total anarchy, with khans being enthroned and murdered in rapid succession.

By the middle of the nineteenth century, the political landscape of Central Asia was one of terminal decline. The three Uzbek khanates were locked in a destructive triangle of rivalry. Khiva, isolated and economically dependent on its predatory slave trade, was a state apart. Bukhara, the most prestigious but also the most conservative and stagnant of the three, was consumed by its feud with Kokand. Kokand, the youngest and once most dynamic, had burned itself out in a blaze of over-expansion and suicidal internal conflict. Their endless wars had impoverished their people, disrupted trade, and left them militarily exhausted. They were suspicious of each other, incapable of forming a united front, and largely ignorant of the true scale of the threat that was now massing on their northern frontiers. The gears of the Great Game were turning, and the Russian Empire, patient and methodical, was preparing to advance. The era of the independent khanates was drawing to a close.

CHAPTER SIXTEEN: The Russian Conquest of Central Asia

By the middle of the nineteenth century, the three Uzbek khanates had become an anachronism. While Europe and America were being transformed by the Industrial Revolution, steam power, and telegraph wires, the rulers of Khiva, Bukhara, and Kokand still inhabited a medieval world of court intrigue, slave markets, and cavalry charges. Their endless, enervating wars against each other had left them militarily exhausted and politically bankrupt. They were ripe for the picking, dangerously oblivious to the fact that to their north, a different kind of power—a vast, industrializing, and relentlessly expansionist empire—was beginning to look south with renewed interest.

The Russian Empire's push into Central Asia was not a sudden impulse but the culmination of a centuries-long advance. Peter the Great had sent an ill-fated expedition towards Khiva in the early eighteenth century, and numerous other probes and missions had followed. These early forays were often disastrous, undone by the punishing logistics of the steppe and desert. A major Russian campaign against Khiva in the winter of 1839, for instance, ended in a catastrophe of frostbite and starvation without ever reaching its objective. But by the 1850s, the strategic calculus had changed.

Several powerful motives propelled the Tsar's government forward. The most pressing was frontier security. The vast, poorly defined border between the Russian-controlled Kazakh steppes and the khanates was a zone of constant friction, marked by raids, counter-raids, and hostage-taking. For the Russian military, the only logical solution was to advance the frontier to a more "natural" and defensible line. Economics also played a crucial role. Russian industrialists saw Central Asia as a vital source of raw materials, especially cotton—an interest that became acute after the American Civil War disrupted global supplies—and as a captive market for their own manufactured goods.

Looming over these practical concerns was the grand, shadowy backdrop of the "Great Game," the century-long strategic rivalry between the Russian and British empires for influence across Asia. From St. Petersburg, every British move in India or Persia was seen as a potential threat. From London and Calcutta, the steady Russian advance southwards was viewed as a deliberate march towards the jewel in the British crown: India. While a direct clash between the two powers was unlikely, the contest for buffer states and spheres of influence created a powerful incentive for Russia to secure its position in Central Asia before Britain could make any inroads.

Finally, there was the simple, timeless engine of imperialism: the ambition of the men on the ground. The conquest was often driven not by a clear master plan from the Tsar, but by the initiative of fiercely competitive and glory-seeking generals on the frontier. These men, operating thousands of miles from the capital, frequently exceeded their orders, presenting St. Petersburg with a *fait accompli* that the government felt obliged to accept. The conquest was as much a product of this "forward policy" as it was of any grand design.

The first serious phase of the advance began in the 1840s and 50s, with the methodical construction of a line of forts stretching eastward from the Aral Sea along the Syr Darya river. This brought the Russians into direct conflict with the most aggressive and unstable of the three khanates, Kokand, which regarded the lower Syr Darya as its own domain. The Kokandians fought back, but their medieval army was no match for disciplined Russian infantry armed with modern rifles and supported by artillery. In 1853, the key Kokandian fortress of Ak-Mechet (the "White Mosque") was stormed and captured, a clear signal of Russian intent.

The advance paused during the Crimean War, where Russia suffered a humiliating defeat at the hands of Britain and France. This loss, far from ending Russia's ambitions in Asia, actually intensified them. Blocked in the Balkans and the Black Sea, imperial expansion in Central Asia became a way to restore the nation's wounded pride and military prestige. By the early 1860s, the push resumed with renewed vigor. Two Russian columns began a pincer movement, one advancing from the west along the Syr Darya, the other from the east, out of Siberia. Their goal was to link up and close the gap in the frontier, a process that involved capturing the major towns of Turkistan and Chimkent.

The greatest prize in the region, however, was the sprawling city of Tashkent. A major commercial hub of over 100,000 people, it was technically a possession of Kokand, but enjoyed a great deal of autonomy. The man who would make it Russian was General Mikhail Chernyaev, a fiery and insubordinate officer nicknamed the "Lion of Tashkent." In 1865, acting on his own initiative and with a force of less than two thousand men, Chernyaev marched on the city. Facing a much larger defending army and protected by formidable mud-brick walls, he launched a surprise night assault. In a remarkably audacious and bloody attack, his small force breached the defenses and, after two days of street fighting, captured the city.

Chernyaev's unauthorized conquest created a diplomatic headache in St. Petersburg but was a strategic masterstroke. The capture of Tashkent gave Russia control of the most important economic and strategic center between the steppe and the mountains. It also brought the empire into direct confrontation with the most powerful of the khanates, the Emirate of Bukhara, whose ruler, Emir Muzaffar, considered Tashkent to be within his sphere of influence and had been preparing to seize it for himself. War was now inevitable.

The Emir, confident in his large army and his status as the region's preeminent ruler, declared a holy war. The clash, when it came, was a study in contrasts. At the Battle of Irdjar in May 1866, a Bukharan army of some 40,000 men, a traditional force of cavalry and irregular infantry, met a Russian column of around 2,000 under the command of General Dmitrii Romanovsky. The result was a rout. The concentrated fire from Russian rifles and artillery completely shattered the Bukharan charge. The Emir's army dissolved, its soldiers fleeing the field in panic. The battle demonstrated with brutal clarity the technological and tactical chasm that separated the two sides.

The man appointed to institutionalize the Russian presence was General Konstantin von Kaufman. In 1867, the newly conquered territories were organized into the Governor-Generalship of Turkestan, a vast colonial administration with near-absolute military and civil power vested in its leader. Tashkent was made its capital. Kaufman, the first Governor-General, was an empire-builder in the classic mold, earning the nickname the "Half-King of Turkestan" for the immense authority he wielded. His mission was to pacify the region and formalize Russian dominance.

The final subjugation of Bukhara was his first priority. In the spring of 1868, Kaufman marched on the ancient city of Samarkand, the former capital of Amir Timur. After a brief and one-sided battle on the heights overlooking the city, the Bukharan forces retreated, and the city's leaders surrendered. Kaufman occupied Timur's fabled capital, taking possession of its historic treasures, including a colossal Qur'an manuscript traditionally believed to have belonged to the Caliph Uthman.

The Russian garrison left to hold Samarkand soon faced a desperate struggle. While Kaufman pursued the remnants of the Emir's army, the people of the city, joined by warriors from the surrounding countryside, rose up in rebellion. A small Russian force of just a few hundred men found themselves besieged inside the city's ancient citadel. For nearly a week, they fought off wave after wave of attackers in a heroic and bloody defense that became one of the most celebrated episodes of the conquest. They were on the verge of being overwhelmed when Kaufman's returning army broke the siege.

The failed uprising sealed the Emir's fate. Crushed by his defeats and facing rebellion at home, Emir Muzaffar had no choice but to sue for peace. The resulting treaty of 1868 was not one of outright annexation. The Emirate of Bukhara was allowed to continue to exist, and the Emir retained control over his internal affairs. But he was forced to cede Samarkand and other territories, pay a massive indemnity, and grant Russian merchants extensive privileges. Crucially, he had to accept the status of a Russian protectorate, surrendering control of his foreign policy to St. Petersburg. The once-proud Emirate was now a vassal state.

With Kokand neutered and Bukhara subjugated, only one of the three khanates remained independent: Khiva. Isolated in its desert oasis, the Khanate of Khiva had long been a thorn in Russia's side, notorious for its slave markets and for holding Russian subjects in bondage. Kaufman, believing that a state built on slavery had no right to exist, planned a final, decisive campaign to eliminate it. The invasion of Khiva in 1873 was a monumental logistical undertaking. To ensure success and overwhelm the Khivans, five separate Russian columns, totaling over 12,000 men, advanced on the oasis simultaneously from different directions—from Tashkent, Orenburg, and the Caspian Sea.

The campaign was a war against the desert as much as against the Khivans. The columns endured sandstorms, searing heat, and a desperate lack of water. But the careful planning paid off. While some detachments suffered terribly, the main forces converged on the capital as planned. The Khan's army, demoralized and terrified by the multi-pronged invasion, mounted only a token resistance. In May 1873, Russian cannons breached the walls of Khiva, and the city surrendered.

The conquest of Khiva followed the Bukharan model. A treaty was signed that formally abolished the slave trade, a key Russian objective. The Khan was forced to cede territory, pay a war indemnity, and, like the Emir of Bukhara, accept the status of a Russian protectorate. This left only the rump state of the Khanate of Kokand, which had been allowed to fester under the unstable rule of Khudayar Khan. A series of popular uprisings, fueled by high taxes and resentment against Russian encroachment, finally gave Kaufman the pretext he needed for a final annexation. In 1876, after crushing the last vestiges of resistance, the Khanate of Kokand was formally abolished, and its territory was incorporated directly into the Governor-Generalship of Turkestan.

The final piece of the puzzle lay to the south, in the desert lands of modern Turkmenistan. The fierce and independent Turkmen tribes had never been part of the Uzbek khanates and represented the last major pocket of resistance to Russian rule. The task of subduing them fell to General Mikhail Skobelev, a charismatic and utterly ruthless commander known as the "White General." The decisive confrontation came at the massive desert fortress of Geok-Tepe. In January 1881, after a long siege, Russian troops stormed the fortress. The victory was followed by a horrific massacre, as the Russian army, under Skobelev's orders, pursued and slaughtered not only the fleeing Turkmen warriors but thousands of civilians as well.

The fall of Geok-Tepe broke the back of Turkmen resistance and completed the Russian conquest of Central Asia. The establishment of the Transcaspian Oblast secured the border with Persia and brought the Russian Empire to the frontiers of Afghanistan, the buffer state at the very heart of the Great Game. In less than three decades, the political map of the region had been fundamentally and irrevocably redrawn. The age of the independent khanates, which had stretched back to the successors of Timur and Genghis Khan, was over. Mawarannahr, Khwarazm, and Ferghana were now collectively known as Russian Turkestan, provinces in a vast European empire, their fate now tied to the whims and fortunes of a distant Tsar in St. Petersburg.

CHAPTER SEVENTEEN: Life Under Tsarist Rule and the Jadidist Movement

The fall of the great fortress at Geok-Tepe in 1881 did not just mark the end of Turkmen resistance; it signaled the end of an entire epoch. For the first time since the Arab conquests over a millennium earlier, the lands of Mawarannahr, Khwarazm, and Ferghana were not ruled by a sovereign Islamic power, but by a Christian one from Europe. The khans and emirs, who traced their lineage and legitimacy to the world-conquering traditions of Genghis Khan and Amir Timur, were now either deposed, exiled, or reduced to the status of pampered vassals. Their world of tribal levies, Silk Road caravans, and madrasa scholarship was being irrevocably supplanted by a new order of railways, cotton plantations, and Russian garrisons. Life under the Tsar was to be a disorienting experience of profound transformation, one that would simultaneously preserve the old ways while forcibly introducing a strange and powerful new modernity.

The administrative structure imposed by St. Petersburg was a pragmatic, two-tiered system. The lands of the former Khanate of Kokand, along with the strategic cities of Tashkent and Samarkand, were annexed outright and formed the core of the new Governor-Generalship of Turkestan. This vast territory was placed under direct military rule, with Tashkent as its new, grand capital. The Governor-General, an immensely powerful figure often referred to as the "Half-King," wielded near-dictatorial authority over his domain. The first and most famous of these was General Konstantin von Kaufman, an architect of empire who understood that his primary mission was to ensure stability and secure the region for the Tsar. The Emirate of Bukhara and the Khanate of Khiva, however, were allowed to continue as protectorates. Their rulers retained their thrones and titles and were granted full autonomy over the internal affairs of their subjects, but their foreign policy was dictated by Russia, and their continued existence was entirely dependent on the goodwill of the Governor-General. It was a classic colonial arrangement, allowing Russia to control the entire region without the expense and difficulty of directly administering every last town and village.

Initially, the Tsarist policy towards its new Muslim subjects was one of cautious non-interference, particularly in matters of religion and local custom. Kaufman and his successors were acutely aware that they were a small Christian minority ruling over a vast and devoutly Muslim population. Their goal was to pacify, not to provoke. They had no interest in a campaign of Christianization or Russification, which they knew would only lead to rebellion. Sharia courts, presided over by local *qadis* (judges), were permitted to continue settling civil disputes like marriage, divorce, and inheritance according to Islamic law. The great madrasas of Bukhara continued to function, and the power of the conservative clergy over the daily lives of the people was left largely untouched. This policy, described by Kaufman as one of "ignoring" Islam, created a bifurcated reality. A new Russian legal and administrative system was superimposed on the old order, but for most people, day-to-day life continued to be governed by the familiar rhythms of the mosque, the mahalla (neighborhood), and the bazaar.

This hands-off approach to culture did not extend to the economy. The primary reason for the conquest, beyond imperial prestige and the Great Game, was economic exploitation, and the key to this was a single, thirsty crop: cotton. The American Civil War of the 1860s had devastated the textile mills of Moscow and St. Petersburg by cutting off their primary source of raw cotton. Turkestan, with its hot, dry climate and long history of irrigated agriculture, was seen as the perfect solution—a secure, domestic source that would make the Russian textile industry self-sufficient. A massive, state-sponsored effort was launched to transform the region into the empire's cotton basket. American varieties of cotton, which had a longer fiber and were more suited to industrial machinery, were introduced. Peasants were coerced, through a combination of tax incentives and outright pressure, to abandon the cultivation of traditional food crops like wheat and rice in favor of planting cotton.

To move this "white gold" from the fields of Ferghana to the factories of European Russia, a feat of modern engineering was required. The answer was the Trans-Caspian Railway. Beginning in the 1880s on the shores of the Caspian Sea, the "iron steed" pushed steadily eastward across the burning sands of the Karakum desert. It reached Bukhara and Samarkand in 1888, an event that was met with a mixture of awe and apprehension by the local population. By 1899, the line had reached Tashkent, firmly connecting the heart of Central Asia to the industrial core of the empire. The railway was a revolutionary force. It allowed for the rapid movement of troops, cementing Russian military control. It flooded the local bazaars with cheap Russian manufactured goods—textiles, kerosene, sugar, metal tools—which crippled many local artisans. Above all, it enabled the bulk export of cotton on an industrial scale, binding the economy of Turkestan inextricably to that of Russia. The region was being transformed into a colonial monoculture, dangerously dependent on a single cash crop and on grain imported from Russia to feed its own people.

This new economic and political reality brought with it a new population. In the wake of the soldiers came an army of Russian administrators, engineers, merchants, bankers, and workers. This influx of Slavic settlers led to the creation of a peculiar dual urban landscape that became the hallmark of the Tsarist era. Alongside the ancient, labyrinthine "old cities," with their narrow, winding alleys, mud-brick houses, and bustling mosques, the Russians built entirely new "new cities." These Russian quarters were laid out on a grid pattern, with wide, tree-lined boulevards, brick houses with tin roofs, Orthodox churches with their distinctive onion domes, and all the administrative buildings of a European colonial power: the governor's residence, the military barracks, the state bank. The new city and the old city were two different worlds, existing side-by-side but with minimal interaction, a physical manifestation of the colonial divide between the conqueror and the conquered.

It was within this environment of profound change and cultural dislocation that a new intellectual movement began to stir among the native population. It was not a call for violent rebellion, but a call for radical self-reflection and reform. Its proponents became known as the Jadids, from the Arabic phrase *usul-i jadid*, meaning "the new method." They were a small, scattered group of intellectuals, merchants, and enlightened clergy who had come to a painful conclusion: their society had grown stagnant and weak, and this was why it had fallen so easily to the Russians. The only way to survive and to one day regain control of their own destiny was not to reject the modern world, but to embrace it, to learn its secrets, and to reform their own culture from within.

The intellectual godfather of the movement was Ismail Gasprinsky, a Crimean Tatar thinker whose influential newspaper, *Terciman* ("The Interpreter"), was read avidly by the educated few across the Russian Empire's Muslim lands. Gasprinsky argued that the Turkic peoples needed to modernize through education. He championed the "new method" of teaching in schools, which involved abandoning the centuries-old practice of rote memorization of the Qur'an in favor of a phonetic method for learning to read, combined with a modern curriculum that included secular subjects like arithmetic, geography, and history. This, he argued, would create a new generation of Muslims who were both faithful to their religion and equipped to navigate the challenges of the modern world.

In Turkestan, these ideas found fertile ground. The leading figure to emerge was Mahmud Khoja Behbudi, a scholar, writer, and publisher from Samarkand. Behbudi was a man of immense energy and vision who traveled widely, absorbing ideas from Istanbul, Cairo, and other centers of Islamic reform. He argued passionately that the traditional *maktabs* (primary schools) and madrasas were failing the people, producing graduates who were ill-equipped for anything beyond reciting prayers. He and his fellow Jadids began to establish their own "new method" schools, often in the face of intense opposition. These schools were a radical departure, teaching a broad curriculum and often including the Russian language, which the Jadids saw as a necessary tool for understanding and dealing with the ruling power.

The Jadidist project went far beyond school reform. It was a comprehensive program for cultural renewal. They sought to create a modern, standardized literary language based on the local Turkic dialects, an ancestor of modern Uzbek. Behbudi launched one of the first native-language newspapers, *Samarkand*, and a highly influential journal called *Oyna* ("The Mirror"), which became a platform for Jadid ideas on everything from science and hygiene to women's education and the evils of corruption. A new art form, theater, was introduced as a tool for social commentary. Behbudi's own play, *Padarkush* ("The Patricide"), first staged in 1913, was a powerful morality tale about a young man from a wealthy family who, because of his ignorance and lack of a modern education, falls into a life of debauchery and ends up murdering his own father. The message was clear: the old ways, if left unreformed, would lead to self-destruction.

The Jadids saw themselves not as heretics but as true reformers of Islam. Figures like Abdurauf Fitrat, a brilliant young intellectual from Bukhara, argued that the core principles of Islam were perfectly compatible with reason and scientific inquiry. The problem, they contended, was not the faith itself, but the centuries of ignorant and self-serving interpretations layered on top of it by a conservative and corrupt clergy. They sought to purify their religion and their society, to rediscover a dynamic and forward-looking Islam that could serve as the foundation for national progress.

This ambitious agenda placed the Jadids in a perilous position, caught between two immensely powerful and hostile forces. Their most immediate and implacable enemies were the traditionalist clergy and the conservative establishment, who became known as the *Qadimists*, or proponents of the "old method." The ulama saw the Jadids as dangerous apostates who were importing infidel ideas from Russia, undermining the foundations of the faith, and threatening their own long-held monopoly on knowledge and social authority. From the pulpits of the great mosques of Bukhara and Tashkent, they denounced the Jadids, declared their schools to be dens of heresy, and warned the people to shun them. This made the work of the reformers incredibly difficult, restricting their influence to a small, educated, urban elite.

At the same time, the Tsarist authorities viewed the Jadids with growing suspicion. While some local Russian officials initially saw the movement as a potentially modernizing and "civilizing" force, the secret police, the *Okhrana*, began to see a more subversive potential. They feared that the Jadids' calls for cultural renewal and their connections to other reform movements in the Ottoman Empire and the Crimea were manifestations of Pan-Turkism and Pan-Islamism—ideologies that could unite the Tsar's Muslim subjects and pose a direct threat to the integrity of the empire. Consequently, Jadid schools were frequently harassed and shut down, their newspapers were heavily censored, and their leaders were placed under surveillance.

By the second decade of the twentieth century, life in Turkestan was a tense tableau of contradictions. The colonial order seemed secure, held in place by railways and garrisons. The cotton economy was booming, enriching the Russian state and a small class of local collaborators. The traditional Islamic establishment, protected by the state's policy of non-interference, remained deeply entrenched. And squeezed between these two powerful forces was the small, beleaguered but determined group of Jadid reformers, arguing for a "third way"—a path of modernity and renewal that was neither slavish imitation of the West nor blind adherence to the past. The illusion of colonial stability, however, was about to be shattered. The strains of the First World War would soon push the empire to its breaking point, culminating in a massive, violent uprising in 1916 that would plunge the entire region into a new era of chaos and conflict, setting the stage for the even greater storm of revolution that was gathering just over the horizon.

CHAPTER EIGHTEEN: The Russian Revolution and the Basmachi Revolt

The carefully constructed edifice of Tsarist colonial rule, which had seemed so permanent and unshakeable, was built on a foundation of suppressed resentment. For fifty years, the peoples of Turkestan had endured foreign domination, economic exploitation, and the casual condescension of their new masters. The illusion of stability was shattered not by a gradual erosion, but by a sudden, violent explosion. The catalyst was a seemingly innocuous decree issued in the summer of 1916. The Russian Empire, bleeding profusely on the battlefields of the First World War, was desperately short of manpower. On June 25, Tsar Nicholas II ordered the mobilization of the empire's "alien" populations, including the Muslims of Central Asia, for labor duties in the rear.

For the people of Turkestan, this was the final indignity. They had been conquered, their lands had been given over to Russian settlers, and their economy had been reoriented to serve the needs of Moscow's textile mills. Now, they were being conscripted to serve in a distant, incomprehensible war that was not their own. The reaction was immediate and ferocious. From the Ferghana Valley to the Semirechye region, a spontaneous and massive uprising engulfed the entire territory. Mobs attacked Russian administrative offices, burned records, and murdered colonial officials. The revolt was particularly savage in the area around Jizzakh, where rebels tore up railway tracks and sought to isolate the Russian garrisons.

The Tsarist response was one of overwhelming and indiscriminate brutality. Punitive columns were dispatched with orders to suppress the rebellion without mercy. Villages were burned, and entire communities were massacred. In the chaos, long-simmering ethnic tensions erupted, with Kyrgyz and Kazakh nomads attacking Russian and Ukrainian peasant settlements, which in turn led to brutal reprisals by settler militias. By the time the revolt was crushed in a welter of blood, tens, perhaps hundreds, of thousands of Central Asians were dead, and a comparable number had fled over the mountains into China to escape the slaughter. The 1916 Uprising was a catastrophe, but it was also a turning point. It had broken the spell of Russian invincibility and created a new generation of leaders radicalized by the experience of armed struggle. The land was saturated with a bitterness that the coming storm of revolution would whip into a fire.

Less than six months after the last embers of the revolt were stamped out, the entire imperial structure that had ordered the suppression simply vanished. In February 1917, revolution erupted in Petrograd, and Tsar Nicholas II abdicated. The news, when it reached Tashkent via the telegraph, created a power vacuum and a wave of political euphoria. For a moment, anything seemed possible. The Jadid reformers, who had been hounded and censored by the Tsarist police, emerged from the shadows, hailing the revolution as a dawn of freedom and opportunity for their people. They quickly formed political organizations, the most important of which was the *Shura-i Islamia* (Islamic Council), to represent the interests of the Muslim population.

Power in Turkestan, however, became dangerously divided. The official authority was the Turkestan Committee, a body appointed by the new Provisional Government in Petrograd and composed of a mixture of liberal Russian officials and a few token, conservative local elites. The real power, however, lay with a far more radical institution: the Tashkent Soviet of Soldiers' and Workers' Deputies. This council was dominated by Russian railway workers, soldiers from the local garrison, and Slavic settlers, many of whom were members of the Bolshevik and Socialist-Revolutionary parties. They had little interest in the nationalist aspirations of the Jadids and were primarily concerned with securing their own privileged position in the colonial hierarchy. They saw the Muslim population not as partners in revolution, but as a backward, counter-revolutionary mass to be controlled.

This fundamental disconnect between the aspirations of the native population and the interests of the Russian workers and soldiers in

Tashkent came to a head with the second, more decisive, revolutionary wave. In October 1917, the Bolsheviks, led by Vladimir Lenin, seized power in Petrograd. The Tashkent Soviet, hearing the news, followed suit. In a brief but bloody struggle, Bolshevik-led Red Guards overthrew the authority of the Provisional Government's Turkestan Committee and declared themselves the supreme power in the land. When the Muslim leaders, including the Jadids, approached the victorious Tashkent Soviet and requested representation for the native population in the new government, they were contemptuously rebuffed. In a decision of profound and lasting arrogance, the Third Regional Congress of Soviets declared that Muslims were to be excluded from all positions of power in the new Turkestan Autonomous Soviet Socialist Republic, citing their supposed political backwardness.

For the Jadids, this was the ultimate betrayal. They had supported the revolution in the hope of achieving a modern, autonomous, and self-governing state. Instead, one form of colonial rule had simply been replaced by another, even more ideologically rigid one. Refusing to accept the legitimacy of the all-Russian Tashkent Soviet, the Muslim political leaders convened their own assembly, the Fourth Extraordinary All-Muslim Congress, in the ancient city of Kokand in the Ferghana Valley. On November 27, 1917, in a direct challenge to the Bolsheviks in Tashkent, the delegates declared the formation of the Turkestan Autonomy, popularly known as the "Kokand Autonomy."

This was the Jadidist dream made manifest. A provisional government was formed, with the respected reformer Muhammadjon Tynyshpaev as its prime minister, later succeeded by Mustafa Chokai. It was to be a modern, secular, democratic state, a republic that would govern in the interests of the native peoples of Turkestan while remaining a part of a wider, federated Russia. They began the difficult work of creating an administration, raising an army, and seeking recognition. For a few short weeks, it seemed that a new kind of Central Asian state might be born.

The Bolsheviks in Tashkent viewed the Kokand Autonomy not as a partner in a federal system, but as an existential, counter-revolutionary threat—a *bourgeois-nationalist* entity that challenged their monopoly on power. They were determined to crush it. In February 1918, a force of Red Army soldiers, composed mainly of Russian troops from the Tashkent garrison, was dispatched to Kokand. They were accompanied by detachments of Armenian Dashnaks, refugees from Ottoman Turkey who harbored a deep animosity towards Turkic peoples. The forces of the Kokand Autonomy, poorly armed and hastily organized, were no match for the disciplined Red Guards.

The fall of Kokand was not just a military defeat; it was a massacre. For three days, the city was given over to a brutal sack. Red Army and Dashnak troops went on a rampage of killing, looting, and burning. Thousands of civilians were slaughtered, and much of the ancient city was destroyed by fire. The brutal suppression of the Kokand Autonomy was a political catastrophe for the Bolsheviks. It demonstrated with shocking clarity that their revolution was, in practice, a Russian-dominated affair that had no place for Muslim self-determination. The bloodbath at Kokand extinguished the hopes of the Jadids for a peaceful, political solution and served as the spark that ignited a widespread, violent, and protracted armed resistance movement across the region. The Soviets would call the men who took up arms *Basmachi*—a derogatory term meaning "bandits." The fighters, however, saw themselves as *mujahideen*, holy warriors fighting for their faith, their land, and their freedom.

The Basmachi revolt was not a unified, centrally commanded nationalist uprising. It was a complex, decentralized, and often chaotic insurgency with many different actors and motivations. It began in the Ferghana Valley, the heartland of the rebellion, where the memory of the Kokand massacre was freshest. Local leaders, known as *qorbashi* (commanders), raised armed bands to defend their villages from the marauding Red Army and the brutal policy of "War Communism," which involved the forced requisitioning of grain, cotton, and livestock from the peasantry. These early Basmachi bands were often a mixture of pious Muslims defending their way of life, peasants enraged by economic policies, and former soldiers from the Kokand Autonomy.

One of the most effective early leaders was Madamin Beg, a former officer who managed to form a temporary and unlikely alliance with a Russian peasant army that was also fighting against the Bolsheviks. For a time, they controlled large swathes of the Ferghana Valley, establishing a provisional government and posing a serious threat to Soviet power. The movement soon spread beyond Ferghana. In the region of Bukhara and Samarkand, other bands emerged, often led by tribal chieftains or charismatic local figures. The Emir of Bukhara, Alim Khan, who had been a Russian vassal, attempted to use the chaos to reassert his independence. After the Red Army under the command of Mikhail Frunze stormed and captured Bukhara in 1920, the deposed Emir fled to the eastern mountains and declared his support for the Basmachi, giving the movement a symbol of traditional legitimacy.

The nature of the fighting was classic guerrilla warfare. The Basmachi, with their superior knowledge of the local terrain and the support of much of the rural population, would launch surprise raids on Soviet garrisons, supply columns, and government officials before melting back into the mountains or countryside. The Red Army responded with overwhelming force and brutal counter-insurgency tactics. Villages suspected of harboring rebels were destroyed, and summary executions were common. For several years, a vicious cycle of raid and reprisal engulfed the region, causing immense suffering for the civilian population caught in the middle.

The rebellion received a dramatic, if ultimately ill-fated, boost in 1921 with the arrival of one of the most famous and controversial figures of the era: Enver Pasha. A former leader of the Ottoman Empire's Young Turk government and a principal architect of its entry into World War I, Enver had fled to Russia after the Ottoman defeat. He was a charismatic, dashing, and hopelessly romantic adventurer with a grand vision of uniting all the Turkic peoples of Asia into a single great empire, a Pan-Turkic dream. Initially, he traveled to Central Asia on a mission for the Bolsheviks, who hoped he could use his prestige to persuade the Basmachi to lay down their arms.

Enver, however, had other plans. Seeing an opportunity to realize his own ambitions, he betrayed his Soviet patrons and defected to the Basmachi. He quickly established himself as the commander-in-chief of all the rebel forces, issuing proclamations in the name of the "Army of Islam." His charisma and military experience breathed new life into the movement. He succeeded, for a time, in uniting many of the disparate bands, capturing Dushanbe, and posing a direct threat to Bukhara. For a brief, heady period in early 1922, it seemed as if Enver's grand ambition might just be achievable.

His success, however, was his undoing. His arrogant, top-down leadership style and his Pan-Turkic ideology alienated many of the local *qorbashi*, who were fighting for local autonomy, not for a new Turkish empire. They resented taking orders from an outsider. The deposed Emir of Bukhara also grew deeply suspicious of Enver's ambitions, fearing he intended to create his own sultanate. Furthermore, Enver's dramatic rise forced the Bolsheviks to recognize the gravity of the threat. A massive Red Army force, equipped with modern artillery and aircraft, was sent to hunt him down. In August 1922, near the village of Ab-i-Dara in modern-day Tajikistan, Enver's small detachment was cornered. In a final, suicidal cavalry charge against machine-gun positions, the great adventurer was killed.

The death of Enver Pasha was a mortal blow to the Basmachi revolt as a unified movement. It deprived the rebellion of its most famous international figure and its only plausible unifying leader. The movement fractured back into its constituent local parts, making it easier for the Soviets to defeat them piecemeal. The Bolsheviks also began to employ a more sophisticated strategy, combining the stick of military force with the carrot of political and economic concessions. The introduction of the New Economic Policy (NEP) in 1921 ended the hated grain requisitions, replacing them with a fixed tax and allowing peasants to sell their surplus.

This did much to pacify the countryside and rob the Basmachi of their core base of support. Land and water reforms were introduced, aimed at breaking the power of the old landed elites who often supported the rebels. Generous amnesties were offered to fighters who surrendered, and a concerted propaganda campaign was launched to portray the Basmachi as British-backed bandits and reactionary religious fanatics who stood in the way of progress.

By 1924, the Red Army had gained the upper hand. The main Basmachi forces in the Ferghana Valley had been defeated or had surrendered. While isolated bands would continue a sporadic resistance in remote mountain and desert areas, some holding out until the early 1930s, the revolt as a major military threat to Soviet power was over. The brutal and chaotic years of war that had begun with the 1916 uprising had finally drawn to a close. The dream of the Kokand Autonomy was a distant memory, and the resistance of the Basmachi had been crushed. The land was pacified, but it was also exhausted and traumatized. The stage was now set for the Bolsheviks to consolidate their victory and begin their unprecedented project of social and political engineering: the formal creation of new Soviet nations, carved out of the ruins of old Turkestan.

CHAPTER NINETEEN: The Creation of the Uzbek Soviet Socialist Republic

The final, desperate charge of Enver Pasha in the summer of 1922 was more than just the end of a romantic adventurer; it was the death rattle of an era. With the Basmachi revolt broken and its charismatic figurehead gone, the Bolsheviks were the undisputed, if exhausted, masters of Turkestan. The old order lay in ruins. The Emirate of Bukhara and the Khanate of Khiva, having been toppled in 1920, had been replaced by the short-lived and theoretically independent Bukharan and Khorezmian People's Soviet Republics. The core of the region, the former Tsarist Governor-Generalship, was now the Turkestan Autonomous Soviet Socialist Republic. This chaotic patchwork of new and old entities was a messy, transitional arrangement, a battlefield relic that served no long-term purpose for the new masters in Moscow. The Bolsheviks had conquered Central Asia; now they faced the far more complex task of remaking it in their own image.

The challenge was as much ideological as it was administrative. Classical Marxism had predicted that the fires of proletarian revolution would melt away the supposedly artificial constructs of nationality and religion, uniting workers of all backgrounds in a single, class-based solidarity. The reality of the Russian Civil War and its aftermath had taught the Bolsheviks a harsh lesson: nationalism was not a dying ember but a blazing fire, a force of immense power that could either consume their project or be harnessed to serve it. The architect of the solution was Joseph Stalin, in his capacity as the People's Commissar for Nationalities. The policy he championed was encapsulated in a brilliant, if deeply cynical, slogan: "national in form, socialist in content."

The idea was to preemptively neutralize the appeal of independent nationalism by offering a state-sponsored version of it. The various peoples of the Soviet Union would be granted their own national territories, their own national languages would be promoted as the language of government and education, and their own national cultures would be officially celebrated. Each group would get all the outward forms of a nation-state: a republic, a flag, an academy of sciences, a national theater. The content, however—the politics, the ideology, the economic system—would be uniformly socialist and controlled with an iron grip by the centralized Communist Party in Moscow. It was a grand strategy designed to co-opt the very force that threatened to tear their new empire apart. It would also serve the timeless imperial strategy of "divide and rule," shattering any lingering dreams of a unified Pan-Turkic or Pan-Islamic state in Central Asia by carving the region up into mutually suspicious and sometimes competing national units.

In 1924, Moscow decreed that the time had come to apply this policy to Central Asia. The existing political geography was to be scrapped and redrawn along supposedly scientific, ethno-national lines. This monumental undertaking was known as the National-Territorial Delimitation (*natsional'noe razmezhevanie*). A special commission was dispatched from the center, armed with maps, census data, and teams of ethnographers and linguists, to perform a kind of political surgery on the living body of the region. Their task was to answer a question that many of the inhabitants themselves would have found bewildering: Who was an "Uzbek," who was a "Tajik," a "Turkmen," a "Kazakh," or a "Kyrgyz"?

The reality on the ground was infinitely more complex than the neat categories the commission sought to impose. For centuries, identities in Central Asia had been fluid and layered. A person might identify first and foremost with their family or clan, their neighborhood, their city, or their religion. In the great oasis cities, bilingualism was the norm. An educated merchant in Bukhara might speak a Turkic dialect (what would become Uzbek) in the bazaar and at home, and Persian (Tajik) for poetry, business, and administration, without feeling any contradiction. The distinction between "Uzbek" and "Tajik" was often blurry, a matter of lifestyle—the stereotypical Uzbek being a descendant of nomadic conquerors, the Tajik a member of the ancient settled, Persian-speaking population—as much as a fixed ethnic identity. The Soviet ethnographers, however, were on a mission to create clarity, even if it meant inventing it. They used language as their primary, and often bluntest, instrument. If a village predominantly spoke a Turkic dialect, it was designated Uzbek; if it spoke a Persian one, it became Tajik.

This process inevitably led to bitter disputes, as local elites jockeyed to have their territory included in one republic or another. The most explosive and consequential of these disputes centered on the two most historic and prestigious cities in the region: Bukhara and Samarkand. These ancient capitals were the heart of Central Asian civilization, and for over a thousand years, their high culture and literary language had been overwhelmingly Persian. A large, perhaps even a majority, portion of their urban population was Tajik-speaking. Logically, they should have formed the core of the new Tajik republic.

Yet, when the final maps were drawn, both cities were assigned to the much larger Uzbek Soviet Socialist Republic. The official Soviet rationale was based on economic and demographic grounds. The commissions argued that while the cities themselves were Tajik-speaking islands, they were surrounded by a sea of Uzbek-speaking agriculturalists with whom their economies were inextricably linked. To separate the cities from their hinterlands, it was argued, would be economically unviable. The unspoken political logic, however, was far more potent. The Uzbeks were seen as the largest and most politically significant group in the sedentary heart of the region. To create a strong, viable Uzbek SSR that could serve as a regional anchor for Soviet power, it needed to possess the region's great historic centers. A Tajik republic stripped of its traditional capitals would be a far weaker and less troublesome entity. This decision, more than any other, poisoned relations between the two new nations from the moment of their birth, creating a legacy of resentment that would endure for the rest of the century and beyond.

On October 27, 1924, the old political map was officially wiped clean. The Turkestan ASSR, the Bukharan PSR, and the Khorezmian PSR were all dissolved. In their place, the Central Executive Committee of the USSR proclaimed the creation of the Uzbek Soviet Socialist Republic and the Turkmen Soviet Socialist

Republic. Carved out of the Uzbek SSR was the Tajik Autonomous Soviet Socialist Republic (ASSR), a subordinate entity that would not be elevated to the status of a full union republic until 1929. The Kyrgyz and Kazakh peoples were also given autonomous regions that would later become full republics.

The new Uzbek SSR was a vast and diverse territory. It included the fertile Ferghana Valley, the Zarafshan oasis with its contested jewels of Samarkand and Bukhara, the ancient lands of Khwarazm, and the booming new administrative center of Tashkent. The task of leading this new creation fell to a generation of "national communists"—men who were, for the most part, former Jadid reformers who had thrown their lot in with the Bolsheviks. They were not traditional Marxists, but modernizing nationalists who saw the Soviet project as the only viable path to dragging their society out of what they saw as medieval backwardness. They believed they could build a modern Uzbek nation within the Soviet framework.

The two most prominent figures of this new elite were Fayzulla Khodjaev and Akmal Ikramov. They were a study in contrasts. Khodjaev was the cosmopolitan son of a fabulously wealthy Bukharan merchant, a European-educated Jadid who had financed the anti-emirate movement and who now became the first head of government of the Uzbek SSR, the Chairman of its Council of People's Commissars. He was a pragmatist, a skilled administrator who hoped to manage the transition to socialism with a minimum of destructive upheaval. Ikramov, by contrast, was a man of humbler origins, a committed and zealous communist who rose to become the First Secretary of the Communist Party of Uzbekistan. He was the ideologue, the true believer, the direct line to Moscow's will. For a decade, the delicate and often tense partnership between Khodjaev the statesman and Ikramov the party boss would define the politics of the new republic.

The first order of business was to create the institutions of a modern state where none had existed before. A constitution was written, mirroring that of the Soviet Union. A new administrative map was drawn, dividing the republic into regions and districts. A state bureaucracy was established, staffed at the upper levels by these national communists, but heavily reliant on Russian cadres and specialists in the technical fields. The capital was a moveable feast in the early years. Initially, the government sat in Bukhara, a nod to its historic prestige. In 1925, it was moved to Samarkand, the even grander capital of Timur. Finally, in 1930, it was permanently relocated to Tashkent. This was a highly symbolic move. Tashkent was the new city, the Russian-built center of the colonial administration, the hub of the railway network, and home to the largest concentration of Russian workers and soldiers. Shifting the capital there signaled a decisive break with the old, traditional centers of Islamic learning and a full embrace of a new, Soviet, industrial future.

The creation of the Uzbek SSR was a revolutionary act in the truest sense of the word. It was not an organic development but a deliberate and radical feat of political engineering. For the first time in history, a state called "Uzbekistan" existed with clearly defined borders on a map. This act of drawing lines had profound consequences. It began the process of hardening the previously fluid identities of the region's peoples. An official, state-sanctioned Uzbek nationality was now a fact of life, recorded in new Soviet internal passports. The government, through its control of the new school system and the press, began to standardize the Uzbek language, selecting a particular dialect as the literary norm. A national narrative was constructed, a history written to legitimize the new republic, celebrating figures like the astronomer Ulugh Beg while conveniently ignoring the religious zealotry of others.

The national delimitation of 1924 was a masterpiece of Soviet strategy. It successfully shattered any possibility of a unified Turkestan that could one day challenge Moscow. It created new nationalisms that were entirely dependent on the Soviet state for their existence and legitimacy. It built in sources of friction, like the status of Samarkand and Bukhara or the complex, intertwined borders in the Ferghana Valley, which ensured that Moscow would always be the indispensable mediator in any regional dispute. The new republic was "national in form," with its own language, territory, and native leaders like Khodjaev. Now, the far more brutal and transformative task of filling this new form with "socialist content" was about to begin. The stage was set for the upheavals of collectivization, industrialization, and cultural revolution that would fundamentally reshape the society that had just been willed into existence.

CHAPTER TWENTY: Soviet Modernization and its Impact on Uzbek Society

The creation of the Uzbek Soviet Socialist Republic in 1924 was an act of political cartography on an epic scale, a drawing of lines on a map that willed a new nation into existence. But this new, neatly bordered entity was, in the eyes of the Bolsheviks in Moscow, merely an empty vessel. The far more difficult and brutal task was to fill this "national form" with "socialist content." The decade and a half that followed was a period of revolutionary upheaval on a scale that dwarfed even the Mongol invasion. It was a time of forced-march modernization, a relentless and often violent assault on every pillar of traditional Uzbek life—its faith, its social structure, its economy, and even its alphabet. The goal was nothing less than the forging of a New Soviet Man, an Uzbek in language and cultural flair, but a communist in spirit and a Muscovite in loyalty.

The men initially charged with overseeing this transformation were the very founders of the new republic, the national communists like Fayzulla Khodjaev and Akmal Ikramov. They were former Jadids who had seen in the Bolsheviks a ruthless but effective tool for dragging their society out of what they considered a state of medieval decay. They were modernizers who believed they could build a progressive, enlightened Uzbekistan within the Soviet framework. They would soon discover, however, that Moscow's definition of progress was absolute and that the revolution they had helped unleash would, in the end, devour them as well.

The first and most dramatic front in this war on the old world was the battle for the soul, and the face, of the Uzbek woman. In 1927, on International Women's Day, the Communist Party launched one of the most audacious and violent campaigns of social engineering in its history: the *Hujum*, or "assault." The primary target of this assault was the *paranja*, the heavy, horsehair veil that completely shrouded a woman's body and face, and the *chachvon*, the black net that covered her features. For the Soviets, the veil was the ultimate symbol of female oppression, a portable prison that represented everything they found backward and repugnant in the old society. The *Hujum* was to be a public, theatrical, and decisive act of liberation.

Across the republic, meetings were organized where party activists and Russian women would deliver fiery speeches on emancipation. Then, in carefully staged ceremonies, Uzbek women, often the wives and daughters of local party members, would ascend a platform, renounce the old ways, and cast their veils into a great bonfire. These acts were intended to be inspiring symbols of a new dawn. For the vast majority of the traditional population, however, they were a profound and horrifying sacrilege, a direct assault by an infidel state on the honor of their families and the sacred tenets of their faith.

The backlash was immediate and murderous. The *Hujum* did not just provoke debate; it unleashed a wave of terror. Women who dared to appear in public unveiled were ostracized, beaten, and sometimes killed, often by their own husbands, brothers, or fathers in a desperate and brutal attempt to restore the family's honor. Party activists were assassinated. The campaign turned neighbor against neighbor and ripped families apart, creating a social battleground in every town and village. While the state never officially retreated, the sheer ferocity of the resistance forced a change in tactics. Coercion was gradually replaced by a more patient, long-term strategy of promoting female education and employment, but the violent trauma of the *Hujum* left deep scars on the collective psyche.

Parallel to the assault on the veil was an all-out war on Islam itself. The Bolsheviks were militant atheists who saw organized religion as a rival ideology and the clergy as a class of exploiters. The campaign to eradicate Islam from public life was systematic and relentless. The vast landholdings of the religious endowments, the *waqfs*, which had supported the mosques and madrasas for centuries, were confiscated, bankrupting the entire religious establishment at a stroke. The Sharia courts, which had been tolerated in the early years, were abolished, and all justice was now dispensed by the secular Soviet state.

The physical symbols of the faith were targeted for destruction or desecration. Thousands of mosques and madrasas were closed down. Some were demolished, their bricks used for other construction projects. Others were repurposed with a deliberate, propagandistic irony. The grand Friday mosque in one town might become a warehouse for storing cotton, while a venerable madrasa in another would be converted into an Anti-Religious Museum, its walls now displaying lurid cartoons mocking the Prophet and the mullahs. The clergy, the *ulama*, were branded as "social parasites." Thousands were arrested, exiled to the labor camps of Siberia, or simply executed. The ancient call to prayer, which had echoed across the cities of Mawarannahr for over a thousand years, was silenced.

A more subtle, but perhaps even more profound, act of cultural surgery was the attack on the very script in which the Uzbek identity had been written. For centuries, the languages of Central Asia had been written in the Arabic alphabet, the sacred script of the Qur'an and the medium of a vast and rich literary heritage. For the Soviets, this script was an unbreakable link to Islam and to the pre-Soviet past. To build a new world, the old words had to be unlearned. In 1929, by decree from the center, the Arabic script was abolished and replaced with a new Latin alphabet. This was celebrated as a great leap forward, a step towards modernity and mass literacy. For a decade, an entire generation learned to read and write in this new Latin script.

The experiment, however, was short-lived. By the late 1930s, as Stalin's power became absolute and a new wave of Russian chauvinism swept the country, the policy changed again. Latin was now deemed a tool of "bourgeois nationalism" that separated the Turkic peoples from their Russian brethren. In 1940, another decree was issued. The Latin alphabet was abolished and replaced with a modified Cyrillic script, based on the Russian alphabet.

This second, forced change in just over a decade was a stunning act of cultural severance. Within a single generation, the people of Uzbekistan were rendered illiterate in the script of their grandparents and their parents. The vast library of their own history, poetry, and religious thought was now inaccessible, locked away behind the bars of an unfamiliar alphabet, its study restricted to a handful of state-approved specialists.

While the cultural revolution was reshaping the minds of the people, an even more brutal economic revolution was transforming the land they lived on. In 1929, Stalin launched the catastrophic policy of collectivization. The goal was to destroy the system of private land ownership in the countryside, eliminate the class of prosperous peasants—branded as *kulaks* or, in the local parlance, *bays*—and force the entire rural population into giant collective farms (*kolkhoz*) controlled by the state. This was intended to increase the efficiency of agriculture and, more importantly, to give the state absolute control over the food supply and the production of cotton.

In Uzbekistan, the campaign was carried out with military ferocity. Party cadres and Komsomol youth activists, often Russians or urban Uzbeks with no understanding of rural life, descended on the villages. They were tasked with "liquidating the *bays* as a class." Anyone deemed to be a *bay*—a definition that could be stretched to include anyone who owned a few extra sheep or was simply disliked by the local party boss—was stripped of their land, their livestock, and their possessions. Thousands were arrested and deported to the frozen wastes of Siberia and northern Russia, their families left destitute.

The rest of the peasantry was herded into the new collective farms. The resistance was desperate and widespread. It was a second, more hopeless phase of the Basmachi revolt. Peasants rose up in localized rebellions, assassinating party officials and fighting pitched battles with Red Army detachments. A more common form of resistance was a scorched-earth protest. Rather than hand over their animals to the collective, millions of peasants slaughtered their own livestock. The result was an economic and humanitarian catastrophe. The number of sheep in the republic plummeted by over seventy-five percent. The destruction of draft animals crippled the ability to plow the fields. Famine stalked the land, particularly in the nomadic regions of Karakalpakstan.

By the mid-1930s, the resistance had been crushed. The state had won its war against the village. The traditional structure of rural society, based on kinship and private ownership, was shattered. In its place was a new hierarchy, with the collective farm chairman, a party appointee, as the new master, dictating every aspect of the peasant's life, from when to plant to how much grain they were allowed to keep for their own sustenance. The primary purpose of this new system was not to feed the people of Uzbekistan but to serve the needs of the Soviet textile industry. The cotton monoculture, begun under the Tsars, was now intensified to an obsessive degree. Moscow set impossibly high quotas for cotton production. To meet them, land that had once been used for growing wheat or vegetables was converted to cotton. The great slogan of the era was *za khlopkovuiu nezavisimost'*—"for cotton independence." The independence being sought was for the Soviet Union, but the price would be paid by the ecology and the people of Uzbekistan.

While the countryside was being forcibly reshaped, a parallel transformation was underway in the cities. The first Five-Year Plans mandated a program of industrialization. While Uzbekistan was not slated to become a center of heavy industry like the Urals, significant investment was poured into infrastructure and factories related to its agricultural base. The railway network was expanded. Giant new cotton ginneries, textile combines, and food-processing plants were built, most famously the Tashkent Textile Combine, which was designed to be a model of Soviet industrial might. This created, for the first time, a small but growing native Uzbek industrial working class, a proletariat that had barely existed a decade earlier. New irrigation projects were also undertaken on a massive scale, with huge new canals being dug, often using the forced labor of dispossessed peasants, to bring water to ever more cotton fields.

This entire edifice of social and economic transformation was held together by an apparatus of total political control and, when deemed necessary, terror. By the mid-1930s, the political atmosphere in the Soviet Union had grown dark and paranoid. Stalin, having consolidated his absolute power, began to turn on the very men who had made the revolution alongside him. The Great Terror, the bloody purge of the Communist Party, the military, and the intelligentsia, swept through Uzbekistan with devastating force. Its targets were the national communists, the generation of former Jadids who still harbored some vision of a distinctly Uzbek path to socialism.

Fayzulla Khodjaev and Akmal Ikramov, the two men who had led the Uzbek SSR since its birth, were marked for death. Their past as Jadid reformers, their connections to the old merchant class, and their occasional arguments with Moscow over ruinous cotton quotas were now re-interpreted as evidence of a vast "bourgeois-nationalist" conspiracy. They were accused of being spies for Britain and Germany, of seeking to restore capitalism, and of plotting to sever Uzbekistan from the Soviet Union. In 1937, they were arrested and transported to Moscow.

In March 1938, they were put on display in one of Stalin's most infamous show trials, the "Trial of the Anti-Soviet Bloc of Rights and Trotskyites," alongside other old Bolshevik luminaries like Nikolai Bukharin. After weeks of torture and interrogation, they delivered their pre-scripted confessions. Khodjaev, the suave and educated former millionaire, and Ikramov, the zealous party man, were declared enemies of the people. They were sentenced to death and shot in a cellar of the Lubyanka prison.

The execution of the republic's founding fathers was the symbolic culmination of the purge. An entire generation of native Uzbek political leaders, writers, poets, and intellectuals—anyone with a connection to the old Jadid movement or a hint of independent thought—was arrested and either executed or sent to the Gulag. The Uzbek Communist Party was gutted and then restaffed with a new generation of leaders, colorless and completely subservient apparatchiks who owed their careers entirely to Moscow and whose primary qualification was their unquestioning loyalty to Stalin. By the time the terror subsided on the eve of the Second World War, the project of creating a republic that was "national in form" but "socialist in content" was complete. The national form remained, but any trace of autonomous national content had been systematically and brutally exterminated.

CHAPTER TWENTY-ONE: Uzbekistan During the Second World War and the Post-War Era

The execution of Fayzulla Khodjaev and the generation of national communists in the cellars of the Lubyanka was the brutal capstone of an era. The project to remake Uzbekistan was complete, its leadership purged and replaced by pliant apparatchiks, its culture decapitated, and its economy shackled to the insatiable demands of the cotton combine. The republic, born of revolution and forged in terror, was now a fully integrated and subordinate component of the Stalinist state, its fate entirely in the hands of the Kremlin. That fate, along with the destiny of the entire Soviet Union, was about to be thrown into the crucible of the most destructive war in human history.

When the news of the German invasion of the Soviet Union reached Tashkent on June 22, 1941, it arrived in a land that was already exhausted by two decades of social and economic warfare against its own people. The war, which would be known throughout the Soviet Union as the Great Patriotic War, demanded a new and even more total mobilization. The same state apparatus that had perfected the arts of coercion and mass mobilization for the cotton front and the war against religion now turned its full attention to the war against fascism.

From the cities and collective farms of the Uzbek SSR, a vast river of manpower began to flow westward towards the front. Over the course of the war, approximately 1.5 million people from Uzbekistan were conscripted into the Red Army, representing a staggering proportion of its total male population. These were men who had been born subjects of the Emir of Bukhara or the Khan of Khiva and now found themselves fighting and dying thousands of miles from home in the frozen forests outside Moscow, the rubble of Stalingrad, and the final, apocalyptic battle for Berlin. They served in all branches of the armed forces, with many distinguishing themselves for their bravery. But the human cost was immense. Official figures record that over 260,000 soldiers from Uzbekistan were killed in action, with tens of thousands more listed as missing. Scarcely a family in the republic was left untouched by loss.

While its sons were fighting at the front, Uzbekistan itself was transformed into a vital bastion of the Soviet war effort, a safe haven deep in the rear for the Union's industrial might and its displaced peoples. As the Wehrmacht sliced through Ukraine, Belarus, and western Russia, a frantic, unprecedented evacuation was launched. Entire factories, complete with their machinery, engineers, and skilled workers, were dismantled, loaded onto tens of thousands of railway cars, and shipped east. Uzbekistan became a primary destination for this industrial exodus.

Over one hundred major industrial enterprises were relocated to the republic. The roar of new foundries and assembly lines soon echoed across the ancient oases. Aircraft factories were reassembled in Tashkent, producing Ilyushin transport planes and fighter aircraft. Agricultural machinery plants from Ukraine were converted to produce mines, mortars, and munitions. The republic's own resource base was exploited with a new urgency. Coal from Angren, copper from Almalyk, and oil from the Ferghana Valley were all fed into the ravenous war machine. This was not just a relocation; it was a second, accelerated industrial revolution that fundamentally altered the economic landscape of the republic.

Even more transformative than the arrival of the factories was the influx of people. A human tide of over 1.5 million evacuees and refugees poured into Uzbekistan. They were Russians, Ukrainians, Belarusians, and a significant number of Soviet Jews fleeing the Holocaust. They arrived in Tashkent and other cities, exhausted and traumatized, having lost their homes and often their entire families. This mass migration placed an enormous strain on the republic's resources, which were already stretched to the limit by the war effort. Food and housing were in desperately short supply.

Yet what followed became one of the most celebrated and mythologized episodes of the Soviet era. The people of Uzbekistan, themselves no strangers to suffering and privation, opened their homes and shared what little they had. The phrase "Tashkent—the City of Bread" entered the popular lexicon, a symbol of Central Asian hospitality in the darkest of times. The most poignant aspect of this story was the fate of the war orphans, hundreds of thousands of children separated from their parents in the chaos of the invasion and evacuation. Uzbek families adopted tens of thousands of these children, regardless of their nationality or religion, raising them as their own. The most famous example, which would be lionized in Soviet books and films, was the family of a Tashkent blacksmith, Shaakhmed Shamakhmudov, and his wife, Bahri, who adopted fifteen children of various ethnicities. This narrative of selfless generosity became a cornerstone of the official ideology of the "unbreakable friendship of the peoples," a powerful and genuinely felt story of shared sacrifice that temporarily overshadowed the grim realities of the colonial relationship.

The war also prompted a stunning and deeply pragmatic reversal of state policy on a subject that had been a central battleground for two decades: Islam. Joseph Stalin, the man who had closed thousands of mosques and executed countless mullahs, now understood that he needed every possible resource to rally the people for the defense of the motherland. Patriotism, even religious patriotism, was no longer a crime but a strategic asset. The state's militant atheist propaganda was abruptly toned down. For the first time in years, the official press began to speak of the great Muslim heroes of the past, like Amir Timur, who were recast as patriotic defenders of the homeland.

This new tolerance was formalized in 1943. In a move that would have been unthinkable just a few years earlier, the government sanctioned the establishment of an official governing body for the faith: the Spiritual Administration of the Muslims of Central Asia and Kazakhstan, or SADUM. Its headquarters were established in Tashkent, and its first chairman was a member of a distinguished family of theologians. SADUM was, of course, a state-controlled institution, designed to ensure that the clergy and the faith served the interests of the Soviet regime. Its leaders were expected to issue fatwas in support of the war effort and to encourage the faithful to buy war bonds. But for the beleaguered Muslim community, its creation was a momentous event. It was a partial restoration of their religious institutions and a tacit admission by the state that the war on Islam had, for now, been suspended.

Throughout the war, the primary economic demand placed on the republic remained unchanged: cotton. The need for uniforms, bandages, and gunpowder components made cotton a strategic resource of the highest order. The pressure to meet and exceed production quotas was relentless. With the majority of able-bodied men at the front, the back-breaking labor in the fields fell almost entirely to women, children, and the elderly. They worked from dawn until dusk, often in conditions of near-starvation, their efforts celebrated in the state press as heroic contributions to the final victory.

The end of the war in 1945 brought a wave of exhausted relief, but no real respite. The soldiers who returned—many of them disabled, all of them scarred by their experiences—came home to a land that had been irrevocably changed. The demographic makeup of the cities was different, with a much larger Slavic and European population. The economy was now more industrialized, more integrated than ever into the all-union system. The republic's party leadership, once composed of fiery national communists, was now in the hands of quiet, obedient bureaucrats.

The final years of Stalin's life, from 1945 until his death in 1953, were a grim and paranoid time. The brief wartime relaxation of ideological controls was over. A new wave of political repression, the "anti-cosmopolitan" campaign, swept the country, ostensibly targeting western influences but often having a strongly anti-Semitic flavor. In Uzbekistan, this translated into a renewed emphasis on the superiority of Russian culture, the "elder brother" in the Soviet family of nations, and a clampdown on any expression that could be deemed "bourgeois nationalism." The process of Russification, which had slowed during the war, resumed its steady, patient course.

The death of the dictator in March 1953 was a seismic event that shook the entire Soviet world. The uncertainty and fear that followed his demise eventually gave way to a period of limited liberalization under his successor, Nikita Khrushchev, known as the "Thaw." De-Stalinization began, with Khrushchev's famous "Secret Speech" in 1956 denouncing the crimes and the "cult of personality" of his predecessor. In Uzbekistan, this led to the posthumous "rehabilitation" of many of the purged national communists, including Fayzulla Khodjaev, whose names could once again be mentioned in public.

Khrushchev was a man of boundless, often chaotic, energy, and his reign was marked by a series of grand, ambitious, and frequently ill-conceived campaigns. One of the most consequential for Central Asia was the Virgin Lands Campaign, launched in 1953. The project's goal was to dramatically increase the Soviet Union's grain production by plowing up millions of hectares of previously uncultivated steppe, primarily in northern Kazakhstan. While the campaign did not directly take place on Uzbek soil, its ecological consequences were profound. The new grain belt required enormous quantities of water for irrigation, placing an unprecedented new demand on the two great rivers that fed the region, the Amu Darya and the Syr Darya. The first seeds of the future Aral Sea disaster were being sown.

The Khrushchev Thaw did not extend to matters of faith. After the relative tolerance of the war and late Stalinist years, Khrushchev, a fervent believer in the imminent triumph of communism, launched a new, harsh anti-religious campaign in the late 1950s. The number of functioning mosques, which had remained small but stable, was once again drastically reduced. Religious literature was confiscated, and pilgrimage to local shrines was actively discouraged. The state's atheist propaganda machine, which had been relatively quiet, was cranked back up to full volume.

It was during this period of post-war reconstruction and Khrushchev's reforms that a new generation of native Uzbek leadership, forged entirely within the Soviet system, began its rise to power. These were men who had come of age after the revolution, had served loyally during the war, and had navigated the treacherous currents of Stalinist politics. They were not Jadid idealists; they were pragmatic party men who understood how the system worked and how to work the system.

The figure who would come to personify this new elite more than any other was Sharof Rashidov. Born to a peasant family, Rashidov had a classic Soviet career trajectory: he was educated in a Soviet university, worked as a journalist and editor of the main party newspaper, and steadily rose through the ranks of the Communist Party apparatus. He was intelligent, politically astute, and, above all, a master of cultivating relationships with the right people in Moscow. In 1959, he was appointed to the top post in the republic, the First Secretary of the Central Committee of the Communist Party of Uzbekistan. It was the beginning of a reign that would last for nearly a quarter of a century, a period in which he would become the undisputed master of the republic, a new kind of khan who ruled with the blessing of the Kremlin and whose name would become synonymous with the zenith, and the spectacular decay, of Soviet Uzbekistan.

CHAPTER TWENTY-TWO: The Path to Independence: The Late Soviet Years

For nearly a quarter of a century, from 1959 until his death in 1983, Uzbekistan was Sharof Rashidov. A masterful Soviet politician of the Brezhnev school, Rashidov ruled the republic as his personal fiefdom, a quiet, sun-drenched corner of the empire where the cotton was plentiful and troublesome questions were seldom asked. He was a product of the system, a man who rose from a peasant family to become a writer, a party functionary, and ultimately, the First Secretary of the Communist Party of Uzbekistan. He projected an image of avuncular authority, the wise patriarch of the Uzbek people, the loyal lieutenant of Moscow who could be counted on to deliver. He was, in essence, the perfect regional khan for the era of "developed socialism," a period of comfortable, corrupt, and ultimately unsustainable stagnation.

Rashidov's genius lay in his ability to play a double game. To the Kremlin, he was the guarantor of stability and, above all, of cotton. Every year, he would travel to Moscow to report ever-increasing, record-breaking harvests of the "white gold" that was the republic's primary, and almost sole, purpose in the Soviet economic system. These phantom tons of cotton earned him accolades, medals, and, most importantly, a torrent of subsidies and investment funds that flowed from the central budget into the republic. Back in Uzbekistan, he distributed this largesse through a vast and intricate network of patronage. Loyalty was rewarded with jobs, houses, cars, and a license to look the other way. He was immensely popular, seen not as a colonial puppet but as a clever native son who knew how to work the system for the benefit of his people, a benevolent padishah who protected his realm from the harshest demands of the center.

The entire edifice, however, was built on a foundation of lies and water. The ever-growing cotton quotas demanded by Moscow were physically impossible to meet. So, beginning in the 1970s, the Rashidov administration perfected a system of mass fraud on an epic scale. Local officials would report the harvesting of cotton that never existed. Entire trainloads of cotton bales would be shuttled from one station to another, counted multiple times to inflate the figures. This elaborate system of deception, known as *pripiski*, or "figure-padding," went all the way to the top. It was a conspiracy of the entire republican elite, a collective fiction that kept Moscow happy and the money flowing. Billions of rubles were paid by the Soviet state for cotton that existed only on paper.

The real-world cost of this obsession was an ecological catastrophe of unprecedented proportions. To irrigate the endless fields of thirsty cotton, the two great rivers of Central Asia, the Amu Darya and the Syr Darya, were being bled dry. Vast, inefficient, and leaky Soviet-built canals diverted nearly all their water before it could reach its natural destination: the Aral Sea. Once the world's fourth-largest inland body of water, a vast freshwater sea teeming with fish, the Aral began to shrink at a terrifying rate. Fishing villages like Muynak, which had once been bustling ports, found themselves dozens, and then hundreds, of kilometers from the receding shoreline, their fishing trawlers left to rust in a newly formed desert.

The exposed seabed was a toxic wasteland, a vast plain of salt and chemical residues from decades of pesticide and fertilizer runoff. Fierce winds would whip this toxic dust into the air, creating devastating salt storms that poisoned agricultural land for hundreds of miles around and caused a dramatic spike in respiratory illnesses, throat cancers, and infant mortality among the local population. The shrinking of the Aral Sea was one of the planet's worst environmental disasters, a slow-motion apocalypse engineered by the centrally planned economy's insatiable demand for white gold.

The comfortable, corrupt world of Sharof Rashidov came to an abrupt end with the death of his patron, Leonid Brezhnev, in 1982. Brezhnev's successor was the formidable former head of the KGB, Yuri Andropov, a stern disciplinarian who was determined to stamp out the corruption that had flourished during the era of stagnation. His gaze fell squarely on Uzbekistan. Rashidov died suddenly in October 1983, officially of a heart attack, though rumors of suicide have persisted ever since. His death lifted the lid on the entire rotten system he had built.

What followed was a political earthquake that shook the republic to its core. Andropov, and later Mikhail Gorbachev, unleashed a massive anti-corruption campaign that became known as the "Cotton Affair" or the "Uzbek Affair." A team of high-powered investigators was dispatched from Moscow, led by the zealous and media-savvy prosecutors Telman Gdlyan and Nikolai Ivanov. They descended upon Uzbekistan with the power and fury of a conquering army, determined to uncover the full extent of the fraud.

For the next several years, the republic was convulsed by a sweeping purge. Gdlyan and Ivanov's investigators, known as the "Moscow landing party," arrested thousands of officials, from collective farm chairmen to government ministers and regional party bosses. The entire leadership of the Uzbek Communist Party and government was sacked. Confessions were extracted through intimidation and, reportedly, torture. A series of high-profile show trials were held, revealing a staggering level of corruption that reached the highest echelons of power in both Tashkent and Moscow, even implicating Brezhnev's own son-in-law.

The "Cotton Affair" was more than just an anti-corruption drive; in the eyes of many Uzbeks, it was a national humiliation. The Soviet press, newly liberated by Gorbachev's policy of *glasnost*, or "openness," portrayed the scandal in lurid detail. The stories transformed what was essentially a systemic problem of the Soviet planned economy into a specifically Uzbek national failing. The entire Uzbek nation was depicted as inherently corrupt, clannish, and backward. The purge was seen not as a cleansing, but as a colonial reconquest, an assault by outsiders on the republic's native leadership. The memory of Sharof Rashidov, who was posthumously disgraced and his monuments torn down, was rehabilitated in the popular imagination. He was no longer a corrupt fraudster but a tragic hero who had tried to protect his people and had been hounded to his death by Moscow.

It was into this atmosphere of national grievance and political turmoil that Mikhail Gorbachev introduced his transformative policies of *perestroika* ("restructuring") and *glasnost*. Intended to revitalize the moribund Soviet system, these reforms had an explosive and unintended effect in the non-Russian republics. By allowing for greater freedom of speech and the creation of unofficial political organizations, they opened a space for long-suppressed national sentiments to come roaring back to life.

In Uzbekistan, the initial focus of this new political activity was the most visible and undeniable wound in the republic: the Aral Sea. An environmental movement called *Birlik* ("Unity") was formed in 1988 by a group of prominent Tashkent intellectuals, writers, and scientists. Their initial demands were environmental: to save the Aral Sea, to end the ruinous cotton monoculture, and to improve the catastrophic public health situation in the disaster zone.

Birlik quickly evolved from an environmental lobby into a broad-based popular front, a mass nationalist movement that channeled all the pent-up frustrations of the Uzbek people. Its platform expanded to include a host of political and cultural demands. They called for the Uzbek language to be made the official state language of the republic, for a re-examination of the Stalinist purges, for the restoration of traditional Uzbek cultural values, and for greater economic and political autonomy from Moscow. For the first time in sixty years, a political organization that was not the Communist Party was holding mass rallies in the streets of Tashkent, drawing crowds of tens of thousands and sending a shockwave through the Soviet establishment.

The new openness of the Gorbachev era also allowed the dark underbelly of the Soviet "friendship of the peoples" to be exposed. As the state's repressive grip weakened, long-simmering ethnic tensions, exacerbated by economic hardship and competition for resources, began to boil over. In June 1989, the Ferghana Valley, the most densely populated and volatile region of Central Asia, erupted in violence. A seemingly minor dispute in the town of Kuvasoy between local Uzbeks and Meskhetian Turks—a people who had been brutally deported from their homeland in Georgia by Stalin in 1944 and resettled in Uzbekistan—escalated into a full-scale pogrom. For several weeks, mobs of Uzbek youths rampaged through the valley, hunting down Meskhetians, burning their homes, and killing dozens. The Soviet army had to be called in to restore order and evacuate the terrified Meskhetian population from the republic. The Ferghana riots were a brutal shock, a demonstration of how quickly the veneer of Soviet internationalism could crumble, leaving raw, violent ethnic nationalism in its place.

The combination of a growing nationalist movement in *Birlik*, bloody ethnic violence in Ferghana, and the complete discrediting of the old guard by the Cotton Affair created a crisis of authority in the republic. The succession of weak and compliant First Secretaries appointed by Moscow in the wake of Rashidov's death had proven unable to control the situation. Moscow needed a new leader, a strong hand, a man from the system who could restore order, tame the nationalists, and keep the republic in line.

In June 1989, they found their man. His name was Islam Karimov. A classic Soviet apparatchik, Karimov had spent his career as an engineer and a planner in the state economic bureaucracy before moving into party work, eventually becoming the party boss of the Kashkadarya region. He was not a charismatic ideologue but a dour, tough, and pragmatic administrator who was untainted by the worst of the Rashidov-era corruption scandals. Crucially, he was seen as a man who could be relied upon to use an iron fist when necessary. He was appointed First Secretary of the Communist Party of Uzbekistan and tasked with a simple mission: put the genie of nationalism back in the bottle.

Karimov moved swiftly to consolidate his power. While paying lip service to Gorbachev's reforms, his main priority was re-establishing the authority of the state. He skillfully outmaneuvered the leaders of *Birlik*, harassing the movement's activists while co-opting its more popular and less threatening demands. In October 1989, in a major concession to the nationalists, the Uzbek Supreme Soviet passed a law declaring Uzbek the official state language. In 1990, Karimov had himself elected to the newly created post of President of the Uzbek SSR, creating a powerful executive office that was independent of the day-to-day politics of the legislature.

The final act of the Soviet drama unfolded with breathtaking speed. Throughout 1990 and early 1991, the authority of the central government in Moscow was evaporating as one republic after another declared its "sovereignty," a deliberately ambiguous term that asserted the supremacy of local laws over all-union ones. Karimov, a cautious and calculating politician, was no revolutionary. He had spent his entire life in the Soviet system and was wary of a complete break. In the all-union referendum of March 1991 on the future of the USSR, he campaigned vigorously for a "yes" vote, reportedly warning that Uzbekistan's rivers would run with blood if it left the Union.

The event that forced his hand, and the hands of leaders across the USSR, was the August Coup of 1991. When a group of hard-line communists attempted to overthrow Mikhail Gorbachev and restore the old order, the future of the Union was sealed. The coup collapsed in three days, but it had fatally discredited the central government and demonstrated that the Soviet Union was beyond saving.

Karimov, who had initially hesitated, now understood that the tide had turned irrevocably. To hesitate any longer would be to be swept away by the forces of history. With the Soviet Union effectively ceasing to exist, independence was no longer a choice but a necessity. On August 31, 1991, at an extraordinary session of the Uzbek Supreme Soviet, President Islam Karimov declared the Republic of Uzbekistan an independent and sovereign state. The Soviet flag was lowered from the public buildings of Tashkent. After 126 years of Russian and Soviet rule, the country was, for the first time in its modern history, the master of its own destiny. The seventy-four-year-long Soviet experiment was over, and a new, uncertain era had begun.

CHAPTER TWENTY-THREE: The First Years of Independence under Islam Karimov

The lowering of the Soviet flag over Tashkent on the last day of August 1991 was a moment of profound and dizzying uncertainty. For the first time in 126 years, the land was not ruled from a distant northern capital. But independence had arrived not through a triumphant war of liberation, but through the implosion of the imperial center. The man left holding the reins was Islam Karimov, a product of the very Soviet system that had just collapsed. He was a man with a mandate to restore order, not to lead a revolution. The challenge he faced was immense: to construct a new state, a new economy, and a new identity from the rubble of the old, all while ensuring that the chaotic forces of change did not spin out of his absolute control.

The first order of business was to legitimize the new reality. On December 29, 1991, just days after the Soviet Union was formally dissolved, Uzbekistan held its first-ever presidential election. Karimov, no longer the Communist Party First Secretary but a self-styled father of the nation, was the inevitable candidate. His only challenger was Muhammad Solih, the leader of the democratic opposition party *Erk* (Freedom), a poet who represented the nationalist aspirations of the urban intelligentsia. The outcome was never in doubt. With the full weight of the state administrative machine behind him, Karimov won a resounding victory with a reported 86 percent of the vote. On the same day, a referendum on independence passed with overwhelming support, retrospectively sanctioning the decision made by the Supreme Soviet four months earlier.

With this new popular mandate, Karimov moved swiftly to consolidate his power and neutralize any potential rivals. The brief spring of political openness that had blossomed under Gorbachev's *glasnost* was brought to an abrupt and chilling end. The popular front *Birlik*, which had once drawn tens of thousands to its rallies, was denied registration as a political party and subjected to a campaign of systematic harassment. Its leaders were intimidated, its meetings broken up, and its newspaper shut down. The *Erk* party, despite its participation in the election, suffered a similar fate. Its leaders, including Muhammad Solih, were accused of plotting a coup and forced into exile. Within a few short years, all organized political opposition within Uzbekistan was effectively liquidated. The country was to be a one-man show.

To replace the now-defunct Communist Party, Karimov had earlier reconstituted it as the People's Democratic Party of Uzbekistan (PDPU), which he led and which served as the new party of power. This provided a ready-made institutional framework for his rule, a network of cadres and officials that reached into every corner of the republic. In December 1992, a new constitution was adopted, establishing a strong presidential republic with all the formal trappings of a democracy: a separation of powers, a bill of rights, and a multi-party system. In practice, however, the new political parties that were allowed to register were carefully vetted, state-sponsored organizations that offered no real challenge to the president's authority. Power was concentrated overwhelmingly in the executive branch, and specifically, in the hands of Karimov himself. A 1995 referendum, a favored tool of post-Soviet strongmen, extended his presidential term, cementing his grip on power for the remainder of the decade.

With political dissent silenced, the government turned to the monumental task of creating a new national ideology to fill the vacuum left by Marxism-Leninism. If the people were not to be united by class, they would be united by a shared, and carefully curated, sense of national identity. The new state slogan became "*O'zbekiston – kelajagi buyuk davlat*" ("Uzbekistan – a state with a great future"), a motto that adorned billboards and public buildings across the country. The intellectual foundation for this great future was to be found in a selective reading of the nation's past.

The central figure in this new national pantheon was Amir Timur. During the Soviet era, Timur had been officially condemned as a brutal feudal conqueror, a textbook villain in the Marxist historical narrative. Overnight, he was rehabilitated and elevated to the status of the nation's supreme founding father. A magnificent, larger-than-life statue of Timur on horseback was erected in the heart of Tashkent, replacing a statue of Karl Marx. The new state ideology portrayed Timur not as a ruthless warlord, but as a wise statesman, a patron of the arts and sciences, and the creator of a vast, centralized empire—a historical precedent for Karimov's own strong, centralized state. By claiming the legacy of Timur, the new government was wrapping itself in the glories of a pre-Russian, pre-Soviet golden age, creating a powerful narrative of national pride and historical continuity.

This process of nation-building was accompanied by a cautious and gradual approach to economic reform. While other post-Soviet states, notably Russia, embraced the radical "shock therapy" of rapid privatization and market liberalization, Karimov explicitly rejected this path. Fearing the social and political chaos that such a sudden transition could unleash, he opted for what became known as the "Uzbek model" of state-led, evolutionary reform. The government's stated priority was stability above all else. The old Soviet-era system of state ownership and central planning was not dismantled overnight but was slowly and selectively reformed. Key sectors of the economy, particularly those related to the country's vast natural resources—gold, natural gas, and, of course, cotton—remained firmly under state control. Privatization, when it occurred, was often a murky affair, transferring assets to well-connected members of the new ruling elite rather than creating a truly competitive market.

This gradualist approach did shield the population from the worst of the hyperinflation and economic collapse that plagued other former Soviet republics in the early 1990s. The state continued to provide a basic social safety net, subsidizing the price of bread and other essential goods. But the underlying structure of the colonial economy remained largely intact. Uzbekistan was still overwhelmingly dependent on the export of raw commodities, primarily cotton. The Soviet-era system of production quotas and forced labor in the cotton fields, now rebranded as a national patriotic duty, continued. The state's refusal to make the national currency, the *som*, freely convertible created a thriving black market and discouraged foreign investment, leaving the economy isolated and largely unreformed.

Perhaps the most complex and delicate challenge facing the new state was the question of Islam. After seventy years of militant Soviet atheism, independence was accompanied by a powerful religious revival. Mosques that had been used as warehouses and museums were reopened and restored. New ones were built, often with funding from Saudi Arabia and other Gulf states. Religious literature flooded into the country, and the call to prayer was heard openly once more. For many, this was a joyous and long-awaited rediscovery of their cultural and spiritual heritage.

The Karimov government adopted a dual strategy to manage this revival. It sought to co-opt and control a state-sanctioned version of the faith while brutally suppressing any form of Islam that operated outside its authority. The old Soviet-era Spiritual Administration of the Muslims of Central Asia (SADUM) was repurposed, becoming the Muslim Board of Uzbekistan, a government body that controlled the appointment of imams, the content of sermons, and the publication of all religious material. Official Islam was to be a pillar of the new state, promoting national values and obedience to the government.

Any group that challenged this state monopoly was branded as "extremist" or "Wahhabist" and ruthlessly crushed. The Ferghana Valley, with its dense population, deep-rooted piety, and history of social unrest, became the primary battleground. Independent Islamic leaders who attracted large followings were arrested. Groups that advocated for a more prominent role for Islam in public life were broken up. The state's security services, the inheritors of the old KGB apparatus, waged a relentless and often brutal campaign against what they termed religious extremism, a campaign that frequently made little distinction between violent jihadists and peaceful dissenters.

This security-first approach was profoundly shaped by events unfolding just across the border. In 1992, neighboring Tajikistan plunged into a devastating civil war. The conflict pitted the post-communist government against a loose coalition of democratic, regional, and, most alarmingly for Tashkent, Islamist opposition forces. The spectacle of a neighboring state collapsing into a bloody conflict with a powerful Islamist component became Karimov's foundational nightmare. He saw the Tajik Civil War as a terrifying preview of what could happen in Uzbekistan if he allowed any political opposition, secular or religious, to gain a foothold.

The war had an immediate and direct impact on Uzbekistan. A flood of refugees streamed across the border, and the conflict threatened to spill over into the ethnically mixed areas around Samarkand and Bukhara. Karimov's response was decisive. He sealed the border and threw his full support behind the neo-communist government in Dushanbe, providing military and logistical aid that was crucial to its eventual victory. He also used the war as a powerful justification for his own authoritarian policies at home. The threat of "spillover" from Tajikistan became the constant refrain used to explain the necessity of a strong hand, a powerful army, and a complete intolerance of dissent. Any opposition was framed as an invitation to chaos, a step down the "Tajik path."

As the decade wore on, the state's campaign against unsanctioned Islam intensified. The government's definition of "extremism" grew ever broader, encompassing anyone who wore a beard, prayed outside a state-approved mosque, or possessed unapproved religious literature. Thousands of people were arrested on vague charges of anti-state or anti-constitutional activity. The threat of groups like the Islamic Movement of Uzbekistan (IMU), an organization founded by former Basmachi descendants and veterans of the Tajik war with the stated aim of overthrowing the government, was used to justify this widespread crackdown.

The simmering conflict between the state and its religious opponents exploded into the open on February 16, 1999. On a cold winter morning, a series of six car bombs were detonated across the capital, Tashkent. The targets were key government buildings, and one of the explosions occurred just minutes before President Karimov was due to arrive at the Cabinet of Ministers building. He was unharmed, but sixteen people were killed and over a hundred were injured. The 1999 Tashkent bombings were a profound shock to a country that had prided itself on its stability.

Karimov immediately appeared on national television, blaming the attacks on radical Islamic extremists and vowing a merciless response. The government pointed the finger at the IMU and other underground groups. In the aftermath of the bombings, a massive security sweep was launched. Thousands more people were arrested, and the state's repressive apparatus was given a free hand. The bombings marked a definitive turning point. They shattered the illusion of a peaceful and gradual post-Soviet transition and provided the ultimate justification for the hard-line, security-obsessed state that Karimov had spent the decade building. The first years of independence, which had begun with the hope of national revival and freedom, ended with the grim reality of car bombs in the capital and the consolidation of one of the world's most formidable authoritarian regimes.

CHAPTER TWENTY-FOUR: Navigating Regional and Global Politics in the 21st Century

The car bombs that ripped through the heart of Tashkent in February 1999 did more than shatter the capital's morning calm; they shattered any remaining illusions about a peaceful post-Soviet transition. For President Islam Karimov, the attacks were a grim vindication of the security-first doctrine he had pursued since independence. They provided the ultimate justification for the state's relentless campaign against all forms of unsanctioned Islam, a campaign that now intensified dramatically. The primary external target of the state's wrath was the Islamic Movement of Uzbekistan (IMU), a militant group with roots in the Ferghana Valley that had found safe haven first in the chaos of the Tajik Civil War and later in Taliban-controlled Afghanistan. In the summers of 1999 and 2000, IMU fighters launched a series of armed incursions into the mountainous regions of southern Kyrgyzstan and Uzbekistan, seeking to spark a popular Islamic uprising.

These incursions, while ultimately repelled by the Uzbek and Kyrgyz armies, created a state of near-panic in Tashkent and confirmed Karimov's deepest fears about the threat posed by radical Islam emanating from Afghanistan. The government's response was to turn the country into a fortress. It mined its borders with Kyrgyzstan and Tajikistan, a move that caused outrage among its neighbors and led to numerous civilian casualties over the years. Internally, the security services were given a free hand. Thousands of people were arrested in a sweeping crackdown that often failed to distinguish between violent militants and peaceful believers. This single-minded focus on combating what the government defined as religious extremism became the central, all-consuming priority of the Uzbek state, the lens through which it viewed all foreign and domestic policy.

It was this very obsession that would, unexpectedly, catapult Uzbekistan from a regional pariah into a pivotal player on the world stage. On the morning of September 11, 2001, when hijacked airliners struck the World Trade Center and the Pentagon, the geopolitical landscape of the entire planet was redrawn in a matter of hours. The United States, attacked on its own soil, declared a global "War on Terror." The primary target was al-Qaeda, and its primary state sponsor was the Taliban regime in Afghanistan. Suddenly, the obscure and brutal internal conflict that Uzbekistan had been fighting against the IMU, which was closely allied with al-Qaeda and the Taliban, was no longer a local affair. It was now a central front in a new global war.

President Karimov, a shrewd and pragmatic political survivor, immediately recognized the extraordinary opportunity this presented. For years, he had been telling the world that his country was on the front line against international terrorism, a claim that had been met with considerable skepticism from Western governments more concerned with his abysmal human rights record. Now, the world's only superpower saw things his way. Karimov quickly offered the United States full support. This was not just rhetoric. In early October 2001, even before the first American bombs began to fall on Afghanistan, U.S. troops were on the ground in Uzbekistan.

The centerpiece of this new strategic partnership was the Karshi-Khanabad Air Base in southern Uzbekistan, a former Soviet facility known as K2. With Karimov's permission, the base was handed over to the U.S. military, becoming a critical logistical hub for Operation Enduring Freedom in Afghanistan. U.S. transport planes flew supplies from K2 into northern Afghanistan, and special forces units launched missions from its runways. For the Pentagon, the base was invaluable. For Karimov, the alliance was a political and financial jackpot.

Overnight, Uzbekistan's international isolation ended. In March 2002, Karimov was welcomed to the White House by President George W. Bush, a remarkable turnaround for a leader widely regarded as a dictator. A Strategic Partnership and Cooperation

Framework was signed, enshrining the new relationship in a formal treaty. American military and economic aid began to flow into the country in unprecedented amounts. The Karimov regime, once condemned for its human rights abuses, was now a valued ally. The U.S. government, prioritizing its immediate military needs, significantly toned down its public criticism of the regime's internal repression.

This American embrace, however, was a double-edged sword. While it provided the regime with legitimacy and resources, it also caused deep unease among Uzbekistan's traditional patrons, Russia and China. Moscow and Beijing, while supporting the war against the Taliban, watched with growing alarm as the U.S. military established a long-term footprint in a region they considered their own strategic backyard. Furthermore, the American focus on promoting democracy, however muted, was a source of constant irritation for Karimov, who had no intention of allowing any genuine political reform. He had entered into a marriage of convenience, not a union of shared values.

The inherent contradictions of this alliance were laid bare on May 13, 2005, in the eastern city of Andijan in the Ferghana Valley. The events began with a protest against the trial of 23 local businessmen accused of Islamic extremism. Early that morning, armed supporters of the men stormed a prison, freed them, and took over local government buildings. Throughout the day, thousands of ordinary citizens, emboldened by this initial success, flocked to the city's central square to air a host of grievances about poverty, corruption, and state repression. It was a spontaneous, largely peaceful popular uprising.

The government's response was swift and merciless. As evening approached, security forces, including elite military units, sealed off the square. Without warning, they opened fire on the crowd with automatic weapons and from armored personnel carriers, shooting indiscriminately into the dense mass of men, women, and children. As people tried to flee, they were cut down in a hail of bullets. Eyewitnesses reported that troops then moved through the square, methodically executing the wounded where they lay.

While the government claimed that 187 people, mostly "terrorists," were killed, human rights groups and survivors estimated the death toll to be far higher, with many putting the number at 700 or more. The Andijan massacre was the single deadliest act of state violence against its own citizens in the post-Soviet era.

The international reaction was fractured along geopolitical lines. The United States, the European Union, and the United Nations all called for an independent international investigation into the killings, a demand that Karimov's government angrily rejected. The regime vehemently denied that a massacre had occurred, insisting that its forces had conducted a professional anti-terrorist operation against foreign-backed Islamic militants. Russia and China, in stark contrast, offered their unequivocal support. They accepted Tashkent's version of events and blocked any attempts to launch an investigation through international bodies like the Shanghai Cooperation Organisation (SCO). Soon after the massacre, Karimov was given a red-carpet welcome in Beijing, where he signed a lucrative oil deal.

The Andijan crisis shattered Uzbekistan's strategic partnership with the West. Faced with Karimov's intransigence and mounting evidence of a massacre, the U.S. and the E.U. imposed sanctions, including an arms embargo and visa bans on high-ranking Uzbek officials believed to be responsible for the killings. For Karimov, the Western calls for accountability were an intolerable interference in his country's internal affairs and a direct threat to his rule. His response was decisive. In late July 2005, he gave the United States 180 days to vacate the Karshi-Khanabad airbase. By November, the last American soldier had departed. The brief, intense, and deeply compromised alliance was over.

Having burned his bridges with the West, Karimov pivoted sharply towards Moscow and Beijing. The embrace from Russia and China, which had asked no uncomfortable questions about Andijan, was warm and immediate. Uzbekistan deepened its engagement with the Shanghai Cooperation Organisation, a regional security body dominated by its two giant neighbors.

Tashkent had been a founding member of the SCO in 2001, and the organization's Regional Anti-Terrorist Structure (RATS) was headquartered in the Uzbek capital. Now, the SCO became the primary vehicle for Uzbekistan's international security cooperation. In 2006, Tashkent also rejoined the Collective Security Treaty Organization (CSTO), a Moscow-led military alliance of post-Soviet states, a clear signal of its new strategic orientation.

This re-alignment, however, was not a simple return to Moscow's orbit. Islam Karimov was a fiercely independent and deeply suspicious leader who was fundamentally opposed to any arrangement that might subordinate his country's sovereignty. His foreign policy was often described as "multi-vector," but in practice, it was a form of prickly isolationism, a strategy of balancing the great powers against each other to maximize his own room for maneuver. He was an unreliable and difficult partner for everyone. His commitment to the CSTO was lukewarm at best. He distrusted Russia's neo-imperial ambitions and was wary of being drawn into Moscow's conflicts. In 2012, to the surprise of many, Uzbekistan suspended its membership in the CSTO for a second time, demonstrating its deep-seated reluctance to be tied down in a formal military bloc.

This go-it-alone approach was most pronounced in Uzbekistan's relations with its immediate neighbors. The Karimov era was a period of notoriously poor regional relations. He viewed his country as the natural hegemon of Central Asia and treated his smaller, weaker neighbors with a mixture of bullying and contempt. His relationship with Tajikistan was particularly toxic. The two countries were locked in a bitter dispute over water resources, specifically Tajikistan's ambitious plan to build the giant Rogun hydroelectric dam, which Tashkent feared would give Dushanbe a stranglehold over the Amu Darya river and threaten Uzbekistan's vital cotton crop. Karimov engaged in what was effectively a cold war with his Tajik counterpart, closing border crossings, imposing punitive trade tariffs, and periodically cutting off gas supplies.

Relations with Kyrgyzstan were scarcely better. The undefined and convoluted borders in the Ferghana Valley were a constant source of friction, leading to frequent, sometimes violent, local clashes over access to water and pastureland. In 2010, when brutal ethnic violence erupted between Kyrgyz and the large Uzbek minority in the southern Kyrgyz cities of Osh and Jalal-Abad, Karimov's response was to seal the border, refusing to intervene to protect ethnic Uzbeks and creating a massive refugee crisis. It was a stark demonstration of his state-first, security-obsessed worldview.

Internally, the years following Andijan saw the perfection of the authoritarian state. The system of forced labor in the cotton fields, a legacy of the Soviet era, became even more entrenched, with the government allegedly forcing millions of its citizens, including teachers, doctors, and students, to spend weeks each autumn picking cotton for a pittance. This practice, along with the country's dire human rights record, made Uzbekistan a perennial target of criticism from international organizations. Karimov, however, remained impervious to outside pressure, secure in the knowledge that his country's strategic location and vast gas reserves made him a necessary, if unsavory, partner for the world's powers. He successfully weathered the storm of Western sanctions, which were gradually lifted as strategic interests once again trumped human rights concerns, particularly after the U.S. needed a new supply route for its forces in Afghanistan.

As the years passed, Karimov became an immutable feature of the political landscape, one of the world's longest-serving dictators. He won a series of sham presidential elections with over 90 percent of the vote, cementing his status as the undisputed and unchallengeable father of the nation. By 2016, at the age of 78, he had ruled Uzbekistan for 27 years, first as Communist Party boss and then as president. His final major international appearance was as the host of the Shanghai Cooperation Organisation summit in Tashkent in June of that year.

In late August 2016, reports began to circulate that the president had fallen gravely ill. The government, shrouded in its customary secrecy, remained silent for several days. But the truth could not be contained. On September 2, 2016, after a week of rumor and speculation, it was officially announced that Islam Karimov had died of a stroke. The man who had single-handedly shaped and dominated independent Uzbekistan for a quarter of a century was gone. He was buried in his ancestral city of Samarkand, in a funeral attended by regional leaders and a grieving, uncertain populace. His death created the first genuine power vacuum in the country's independent history, leaving both his own people and the world to wonder what, and who, would come next.

CHAPTER TWENTY-FIVE: The Mirziyoyev Era: A New Chapter of Reforms and Openness

The death of Islam Karimov in September 2016 plunged Uzbekistan into a state of profound and nervous anticipation. For twenty-seven years, he had been the only leader independent Uzbekistan had ever known, a stern and unsmiling patriarch who had ruled through a mixture of force, fear, and carefully managed patronage. The system he built was rigid, isolated, and deeply repressive. His passing created a power vacuum at the very pinnacle of the state, and both domestic and international observers held their breath, wondering if the transition would be a smooth handover or a chaotic, behind-the-scenes struggle for power.

According to the constitution, the head of the Senate, Nigmatilla Yuldashev, was supposed to become the acting president. But in a move that signaled the real lines of power, Yuldashev quickly stood aside. The halls of parliament, in a carefully choreographed session, instead appointed the man who had been Karimov's loyal and largely invisible Prime Minister for the past thirteen years: Shavkat Mirziyoyev. It was a clear consensus choice of the country's powerful elites, including the formidable and shadowy chief of the security services, Rustam Inoyatov, who was seen more as a kingmaker than a king. Mirziyoyev, a man from the heart of the system, was seen as the continuity candidate, someone who could be trusted to maintain the status quo.

What followed, however, was one of the most unexpected political transformations in the post-Soviet world. The man chosen to preserve the Karimov system immediately began to dismantle some of its most notorious and suffocating features. Instead of continuity, Mirziyoyev initiated a dizzying period of reform, a top-down revolution that became known as the "Uzbek Spring." He seemed to understand that the Karimov model of repression and isolation was not just a moral dead-end but a strategic and economic one, a path to inevitable stagnation and collapse.

One of his first and most symbolic acts was to address the human cost of the old regime. For decades, Uzbekistan had been infamous for its long list of political prisoners—human rights activists, journalists, and independent religious figures who had been jailed on trumped-up charges. Mirziyoyev began, cautiously at first and then with gathering speed, to release them. Long-serving and internationally recognized prisoners of conscience, men who had languished in jail for over a decade, were suddenly granted amnesty and allowed to return to their families. While this did not signal a full embrace of political pluralism, it was a profound gesture, a signal that the era of reflexive, paranoid repression was over.

Even more symbolic was the closure of what was arguably the most infamous institution of the Karimov era: the Jaslyk prison. Located in a bleak, remote corner of the Karakalpakstan desert, Jaslyk was a byword for torture and extreme cruelty, a place where political prisoners were subjected to horrific abuse. In August 2019, Mirziyoyev signed a decree ordering its permanent closure. The physical act of shutting down this notorious "place of no return" was a powerful statement that a new, more humane chapter had begun.

The most immediate and tangible change for ordinary citizens, however, came in the form of a revolutionary economic reform. Under Karimov, Uzbekistan's economy had been strangled by draconian currency controls. The official exchange rate of the national currency, the som, was kept artificially high, while a flourishing black market offered a rate that was often double the official one. This system made normal international trade and investment virtually impossible and created a massive opportunity for corruption for those with access to the official rate. In September 2017, in a single, decisive move, Mirziyoyev's government abolished the old system and allowed the som to float freely. The black market vanished overnight. For the first time in a quarter of a century, citizens and businesses could legally buy and sell foreign currency, a move that ripped open the windows of a hermetically sealed economy.

This was accompanied by a broader program of economic liberalization. The government began to simplify the tax code, reduce tariffs on imported goods, and actively court foreign investment, seeking to end the country's long-standing status as a pariah for international business. The goal was to break the old state-led model and transition towards a more market-oriented economy. While the privatization of large state-owned enterprises remained slow and the state's hand in the economy was still heavy, the direction of travel was clear. The "Uzbek model" of isolation was being replaced by a new model of openness and integration.

Nowhere was this new openness more dramatic than in Uzbekistan's foreign policy, particularly its relations with its immediate neighbors. The Karimov era had been one of deep hostility and suspicion. Borders were mined, trade was minimal, and relations with Tajikistan and Kyrgyzstan were in a state of perpetual cold war. Mirziyoyev reversed this policy almost overnight. He declared that Central Asia was Uzbekistan's main foreign policy priority and embarked on a historic campaign of regional diplomacy.

He restored air links with Tajikistan for the first time in twenty-five years and traveled to Dushanbe to sign agreements that began the arduous process of delimiting their long-disputed border. Long-closed border crossings were reopened, allowing thousands of families separated by the fortified frontier to reunite. A similar process was undertaken with Kyrgyzstan, culminating in a landmark 2022 treaty that finally settled the border disputes that had plagued their relations for decades. The minefields were cleared, and the armed checkpoints were replaced with new, modern trade terminals. After a quarter-century of being the region's bully and primary obstacle to cooperation, Uzbekistan suddenly became its most enthusiastic champion, a driving force for regional integration.

This new spirit of openness extended to the wider world. While maintaining a balanced, multi-vector foreign policy that carefully managed relations with the great powers of Russia, China, and the United States, Mirziyoyev's approach was one of proactive engagement rather than prickly isolation. Tashkent became a hub of diplomatic activity, hosting summits and pursuing new trade and investment deals with partners from Europe to Asia. This included a pragmatic and continued engagement with the Taliban government in Afghanistan, recognizing the reality on the ground and the necessity of cooperation on issues of security, trade, and the construction of vital infrastructure like the long-planned Trans-Afghan Railway.

One of the most significant dividends of this new openness was the resolution of an issue that had made Uzbekistan a global symbol of labor abuse: the use of forced labor in the annual cotton harvest. For years, the Karimov government had systematically forced over a million of its own citizens—teachers, doctors, nurses, and students—into the fields each autumn to pick cotton, a practice that led to a widespread international boycott of Uzbek textiles. The Mirziyoyev government recognized that this practice was not only a moral stain but also a major obstacle to economic development. In partnership with international organizations like the International Labour Organization, the government launched a concerted effort to end the system. The active campaign against forced labor led to the eradication of the systematic involvement of state employees and students in the harvest. In March 2022, the Cotton Campaign, a global coalition of human rights groups and brands that had led the boycott for over a decade, formally declared an end to its call for a boycott, citing the elimination of systemic forced labor. It was a major victory for the reforms, opening the door for the country's revitalized textile industry to access global markets.

The reforms, however, were not without their limits and contradictions, and the new era of openness soon faced its most severe test. In the summer of 2022, the government unveiled a draft of proposed constitutional amendments. Buried within the document was a proposal to remove the sovereign status of the vast, autonomous Republic of Karakalpakstan and its constitutional right to secede from Uzbekistan via a referendum. For the Karakalpak people, who possess a distinct language and cultural identity, this was seen as a direct assault on their rights and their history.

On July 1, 2022, what began as a small protest in the Karakalpak capital of Nukus swelled into a mass demonstration of thousands. It was the largest and most serious outbreak of public unrest in Uzbekistan since the Andijan massacre in 2005. The state's initial response followed the old playbook: a heavy-handed security crackdown and an internet blackout. Clashes between protesters and security forces turned violent, and in the ensuing chaos, official figures stated that 21 people were killed and hundreds were injured.

But what happened next demonstrated that this was, indeed, a new Uzbekistan. Instead of doubling down on the repression, President Mirziyoyev did something unprecedented. He flew to Nukus, walked into the heart of the crisis, and spoke directly to the people and local representatives. In a stunning reversal, he announced that the controversial amendments concerning Karakalpakstan would be withdrawn completely. While the crackdown that followed the protests was harsh, with hundreds arrested, the president's personal intervention and public concession to the protesters' core demand was a radical departure from the unyielding authoritarianism of his predecessor. It was a sign that the new government, while still intolerant of disorder, was now at least willing to listen to its people.

The constitutional reform project went ahead without the contentious articles. In April 2023, the new constitution was approved in a referendum. Among its many changes, it extended the presidential term from five to seven years and, crucially, reset the clock on Mirziyoyev's own term limits, allowing him to potentially remain in power until 2040. This raised immediate concerns among international observers that the "Uzbek Spring" might be transitioning into a more familiar pattern of post-Soviet personalized rule. Critics pointed out that while the media was freer and the economic climate had improved, the fundamental political system remained unchanged. Uzbekistan was still a de-facto one-party state with no registered opposition parties and a powerful security apparatus.

The Mirziyoyev era represented a profound break with the frozen, fearful world of Islam Karimov. A country that had been a byword for isolation and repression had opened itself to its neighbors and to the world, releasing political prisoners, liberalizing its economy, and ending the scourge of systematic forced labor. A new generation of Uzbeks grew up in a country where borders were open, where their currency was convertible, and where public criticism of the government, while still risky, was no longer unthinkable. Yet the path forward remained a delicate balancing act. The new Uzbekistan was a place of undeniable progress and lingering contradictions, a society in the midst of a remarkable transformation, still navigating the difficult terrain between the promise of reform and the deep-rooted legacies of its authoritarian past.

Printed in Dunstable, United Kingdom